THE HOLY SPIRIT
IN YOUR LIFE

THE HOLY SPIRIT IN YOUR LIFE

by ANDREW W. BLACKWOOD, JR.

BAKER BOOK HOUSE
Grand Rapids 6, Michigan
1957

THE HOLY SPIRIT IN YOUR LIFE

———————————————

LIBRARY OF CONGRESS CATALOG CARD NUMBER: 57-14662

To
M. A. B.

CONTENTS

THE HALF-KNOWN GOD

*It came to pass, that, while Apollos was at
Corinth, Paul having passed through the
upper coasts came to Ephesus: and finding
certain disciples, he said unto them, Have ye
received the Holy Ghost since ye believed?
And they said unto him, We have not so
much as heard whether there be any Holy
Ghost. And he said unto them, Unto what
then were ye baptized? And they said, Unto
John's baptism. Then said Paul, John
verily baptized with the baptism of repentance, saying unto the people, that they
should believe on him which should come
after him, that is, on Christ Jesus. When
they heard this, they were baptized in
the name of the Lord Jesus. And when Paul
had laid his hands upon them, the
Holy Ghost came on them; and they spake
with tongues, and prophesied.*

ACTS 19:1-6

The Problem in Ephesus

In the days when the church was young, and the secular world seemed fixed and immobile, a conversation took place that has a curious relevance to our day, when the secular world is bursting with a thousand energies, and the church so often seems fixed and immobile. A missionary of Christ came to Ephesus, and there he met some followers of John the Baptist. These were sincere men, who believed devoutly in God the Father, and accepted most of what we would call the Christian code of conduct. What they believed was true, and it was important, but something was lacking. Their faith was sterile.

As the Apostle was probing, to discover what they lacked, he found they had never even heard of the Holy Spirit. Gladly the Apostle brought to these men the whole gospel. When they were prepared, he baptized them in the Christian faith. And almost immediately there was a change. "They spake in tongues and prophesied." When these who had accepted half the gospel accepted all of it, the significant difference was their ability to speak the truth about Christ in a language that people could understand.

The conversation took place in Ephesus, capital city of the land we call "Turkey." In those days it was the Province of Asia, within the Roman Empire. If you were to comb the earth today for an unlikely spot to start a Christian church, you could find no place less hospitable than was ancient Ephesus. This city was known as "The Keeper of the Temple." The temple was dedicated to Diana, a local goddess who had borrowed the name but not the character from Diana, the Roman goddess of chastity. The Ephesian Diana started her slimy career as the Phoenician goddess of fertility: human, plant, and animal. Over the centuries this nature worship degenerated into the worship of lust. The images of Diana that we find today show her as a hundred-breasted monstrosity. Prostitution was an integral part of her worship.

The cult of Diana was so profitable that the temple treasury served also as the Bank of Asia. Naturally there was an alliance between religion and finance. The vested interests had a strong economic incentive to keep Christianity away from Ephesus. But far more serious, the people in Ephesus had an idea of religion that was covered with a thick coat of slime. Anyone could predict, with confidence, that a faith demanding moral purity would be laughed out of Ephesus in short order. When men make these dire and confident predictions, they reckon without the Spirit of the living God.

Twelve sincere men received the whole gospel in Ephesus. And there they stayed, empowered by the Holy Spirit to proclaim the gospel to their neighbors. And soon the twelve were twenty-four. And then the twenty-four were forty-eight. Slowly the cult of Diana gave way. Slowly the church of Jesus Christ grew and developed in numbers and influence. In this unlikely city we find one of the strong churches of the New Testament. The church remained in Ephesus, sending light into the surrounding darkness, until the city itself died. The harbor silted up. Trade was diverted to other ports. The city ceased to be. Only then did the church of Ephesus quit its work. But by that time, the Holy Spirit had started new churches all over the Mediterranean world.

The Problem in Middletown

Picture now an imaginary city in the United States. The more it resembles your home town, the more helpful this picture will be. Call the place Middletown. Fill it with factories. Connect it by rail and highway with the rest of the country. In the center of town place a business district. Surround this on all sides with a residential area, parts of which are already slums, while other parts are heading in that direction. The inner-city population is in a constant flux, as people move out and others move in. Place suburbs at the edges of the city, extending farther and farther into the country. Financially this city is bustling, prosperous, and productive. Does it have any grave spiritual problems?

Although the downtown churches are having a rough time of it, out in the suburbs there is a fantastic growth and development of new congregations. Church building is big business. Further, the new churches are crowded. The past decade has seen a most remarkable growth in the number of those who are professing Christians. The percentage of church membership among the population is at the all-time high. The amount given for religious and charitable purposes likewise is at its peak. Stores that sell only religious books and materials do a thriving business. If one select the evidence carefully enough, one could decide that Christianity has finally succeeded in Middletown, and nobody need ever ask, "The Holy Spirit? What are you talking about?"

Church construction is at the all-time high. And what of divorce? Evidently the bricks and mortar in a church building do not, by themselves, bring the

Spirit of Christ to bear upon the homes in the surrounding community. Churches are crowded on Sunday morning. The rest of the week the juvenile court is crowded. The sale of religious literature reaches new highs. So does the sale of narcotics. In a recent survey of religious opinion, 80 per cent of the people interviewed agreed that the Bible is the Word of God, yet a fourth of the number were unable to name even one of the Gospels. In the seething strife of labor, and the restless tension of class and color, the still, small voice of Christian sanity is seldom heard. Though the golden rule is highly praised on Sunday, it is sometimes ignored on weekdays.

The wide spread of Christianity is not always accompanied by penetrating depth. A rookie policeman in Middletown told his pastor, "My first assignment was to take care of a Bingo game in a church basement. And I stood there, as a guardian of law, while people cashed their relief checks and gambled away their meals for the next two weeks." A layman in Middletown moved to the suburbs and took part in the plans for organizing a new church. He later summarized the arguments: "First: a church will be good for property values. Second: a church will bring down the rates for burglary insurance. Third: if we do not build a church of Denomination X, then Denomination Y will move in and attract a lower class of people." One might guess, from the above mentioned instances, that the financial barrier to the Holy Spirit, so strong in ancient Ephesus, still exists in Middletown. The Lord Jesus has not yet succeeded in expelling the money-changers from the temple.

The church of Christ is more than a building, a budget, and a program. It is supposed to be God's agent on earth to do His will in the community. Christ is the only head of the church. The Holy Spirit is the life-blood of the church. And you are — or ought to be — the hands, feet, eyes, ears, and voice of the church. The church at Ephesus was incomplete. First was a lack of information about God. This could easily be supplied by a competent teacher. More serious was the absence of inward consciousness that God is present. The Ephesian pre-Christians did not yet know the indwelling God, who gives to the Christian direction, purpose, and power to achieve. The Bible describes this reality as the Holy Spirit.

Something is lacking in Middletown. It is not church architecture, budgeting, or program. If these necessary tools could solve problems, there would be no problems left to solve by now. Some suggest that the lack is sound doctrine, others suggest social service, and still others say that the great need is for worship. Each of these is needed. Each, without the others, is incomplete. As Paul found men in Ephesus who had embraced but part of the gospel, so one could find in Middletown those who want only enough religion to give them some peace of mind. They are perfectly willing to use God to achieve their ends, but scarcely enthusiastic about dedicating themselves to achieve God's ends.

Spineless Christianity is widespread in Middletown. What is needed to bring back the vertebrate faith that once smashed the cult of Diana? Where can the church in Middletown find the courage to tackle and the strength to defeat today's idols of materialism, preju-

dice, and greed? The inclusive answer to these
questions is: The church's outstanding need in our
time is to rediscover the Holy Spirit.

Few Christians in Middletown could echo the words
spoken in Ephesus, "We have not so much as heard if
there be any Holy Ghost." It is quite difficult to attend
church without hearing Him mentioned once in a
while. Most Middletown Christians would correctly
define the Holy Spirit as "the third Person of the Holy
Trinity." But if you should ask for an extension of
these remarks, quite frequently you would be told,
"Maybe you'd better go see the minister."

Who Is the Holy Spirit?

The Meaning of Holy. The Old Testament word
that we translate as "holy" has a basic meaning of
"separate." "The holy" is the opposite of the common-
place, exalted beyond the furthest reach of man's
earth-bound thought. The expression "The Holy One"
means "God." It suggests a dividing line between the
divine and the human, that God is God and man is
man. There have been numerous religious attempts to
make God a mere projection of man's thoughts, and
other religious attempts to make man a temporary off-
shoot of God, a divine being in his own right. The
Biblical revelation will have nothing to do with these
ideas; for God is holy.

Holiness meets us as unconditional majesty. Every
attempt to transform Christianity into a religion
of satisfaction and enjoyment is thereby doomed
to failure. Egocentricity masquerading in the robes
of religion is excluded. Faith in God cannot be

measured and evaluated from the point of view of human happiness and needs, even if these concepts be ever so refined and spiritualized. God is not someone whom faith employs with an eye to the higher or lower advantages which he may be able to furnish; nor is he someone we can call upon in order that our needs and desires may be met.

> Gustaf Aulen,
> *The Faith of the Christian Church,*
> United Lutheran Publication House,
> p. 123

As you notice, Bishop Aulen's description of holiness tells us chiefly what "the holy" is not. Speaking in negatives was forced upon him; for the idea of the holy cannot be expressed in the language of daily affairs. Only God is holy.

Only God is holy. Yet in the Old Testament we find a derived meaning of "holy," when something set apart for God is thus described. We see "the holy temple" and "the holy priesthood." In the New Testament the same derived meaning of holiness occurs, as the term is applied to "the holy scriptures" and "the holy faith." Christians, persons who are separated from the world and consecrated to God's service, are called "the holy ones" or "saints." So we see two meanings for "holy." In the basic sense, the word is descriptive of God. In the derived sense, it denotes a person or thing dedicated to God. Christians can use the term "Holy Spirit" in both the above senses. The Holy Spirit is God, in all His mystery, power, and love. But one could also speak of "the holy spirit" as the sensitivity to the divine that God develops within one who is consecrated to

His service. When we read that a person is "filled with the Holy Ghost" (e.g., Acts 6:3), we are to understand that God has taken a special interest in this individual. As a result of God's concern, the human spirit is aware of God's will and determined to do it. A Christian, in New Testament terms, is just such a "holy one," a person dedicated to God's service. You might say that the redemptive work of the Holy Spirit is to make your spirit "holy."

The Meaning of Spirit. Let us now examine the second term. The word "spirit" was once a bold and expressive metaphor, that has gone through a parallel development in many languages. Metaphor is the use of a word or phrase, literally denoting one kind of object, to suggest another object by means of some real or fancied similarity between them. Almost all of the words we use are metaphors that have passed into the language. For example, a few centuries ago our word "pencil" meant the tail of a badger. Then it came to mean a paintbrush, then the line drawn by such a brush, then a similar line drawn with graphite, and today it means the wooden cylinder with a graphite core. What it will mean a century from now is anybody's guess. In its present sense, "pencil" is a dead metaphor, but a live and vigorous word. By contrast, "leech" is a living word that has a living metaphorical meaning. In its basic sense it denotes an obnoxious annelid worm. In its metaphorical sense it means an equally obnoxious type of person. Unconsciously we are talking metaphor, live or dead, almost all the time. The best words with which we can discuss the Holy Spirit are metaphors.

The word "spirit" originally meant "wind" in many

different languages. The four that concern us are Latin,
from which we derive the English word "spirit," German, from which "ghost" comes, Hebrew, the Old
Testament language, and Greek, in which the New
Testament was written. In each of these four diverse
languages, the word for "wind" became a metaphor for
"breath." Then, over a period of centuries, the word
"breath" came to suggest "soul" or "personality." If
ever you have watched while a person was dying, you
can understand how completely natural that metaphor
is. Job uses an expression, natural to him, but foreign
to us, "While my breath is in me, and the spirit of
God is in my nostrils, my lips shall not speak wicked-
ness, nor my tongue utter deceit" (Job 27:3,4). Would
it ever occur to you to say that the Spirit of God is in
your nostrils? The word "spirit" has lost its metaphorical meaning, in English at least. When Jesus says "God
is a Spirit" (John 4:24) we do not even think about
wind and breath. Yet in the New Testament, the same
Greek word "pneuma" denotes alike the wind and the
Divine Being.

When the Authorized Version of the Bible was
translated, the words "ghost" and "spirit" were interchangeable in their meaning. Both meant "personality." In modern English both words have suffered.
"Ghost" has lost its glorious significance. I know some
devout Christians who have completely dropped the
expression "Holy Ghost" from their vocabulary. I am
not willing to go quite that far. But I have found, the
hard way, that "spirit" usually requires a little less
interpretation; so I use it by preference. Of course,
when I quote a passage from the Authorized Version or
any other historical document, I try to quote correctly.

The Holy Spirit means "The Divine Personality."
But this Personality who is God is not the Father nor
is He the Savior. Perhaps I can illustrate the distinction by quoting one of the most beloved prayers
of Christendom:

O God of grace, FROM whom every good prayer
cometh; deliver us from coldness of heart and wan-
dering of mind, that with steadfast thoughts we
may adore Thee, and with contrite prayers we may
obtain that mercy which we need. THROUGH
Jesus Christ our Lord. Amen.

Book of Common Order

The prayer is addressed TO "God of grace." It is
offered THROUGH God the Savior. But it comes
FROM God. God-in-you, enabling you to pray, giving
you warmth of heart and ability to concentrate is what
we Christians mean by "the Holy Spirit."

Symbols for the Spirit

The word "spirit" was originally a daring metaphor
to suggest what cannot be described, the inward working of God. But the Bible is filled with other metaphors
suggesting the same glorious reality. In the opening
words of the Bible, we read, "The Spirit of God moved
upon the face of the waters" (Genesis 1:2). The verb
suggests a bird hovering over the deep. And this symbol
of the Spirit as a bird in flight is found, here and there,
throughout the rest of the Bible.

Another expression, packed with meaning, is "hand."
"By the good hand of our God upon us they brought
us a man of understanding" (Ezra 8:18). The "hand"
of God bears no physical resemblance to the hand at

the end of your arm. The metaphor suggests, with rare beauty and power, the agency by which God puts His creative will into effect.

Another expression has been grievously misunderstood. That is "finger." Again, the "finger of God" bears no physical resemblance to the finger on your hand, even if it were eight miles long. When you are doing delicate, precise work, your fingers are active. So this is a natural descriptive term for God's activity in the world. Moses says, "The Lord delivered unto me two tables of stone written with the finger of God" (Deuteronomy 9:10). Christians believe that the Bible means what it says. What, exactly, is the Bible saying here? The Bible is not concerned with the physical act of engraving the commandments on the stone. The Bible is concerned rather with their source. Do they come from the distilled wisdom of mankind? Do they come from the moral genius of Moses? Do they come through these human agencies? Or do they come from God? The Bible says, clearly and distinctly, they come from God. This dynamic metaphor "finger" has almost died out of use. But it was still natural in Jesus' day. He says, "If I with the finger of God cast out devils . . ." (Luke 11:20). In reporting the same conversation Matthew quotes Jesus as saying, "If I cast out devils by the Spirit of God . . ." (Matthew 12:28). Which term did Jesus actually use, "finger" or "spirit"? There is no way of telling today. It makes no real difference. The terms are interchangeable.

Several other beautiful metaphors for God-who-is-within are found throughout the Bible. He is called the "seal" (II Corinthians 1:22; Ephesians 1:13,14). The allusion here is to a wax seal by which a legal document is authenticated. He is said to be "life" (Romans 8:10). Frequently the Spirit is depicted in terms of water, in its function of quenching thirst (Isaiah 55:1), bringing fertility (Isaiah 44:3), and cleansing (Ezekiel 36:25). The healing properties of oil were doubtless in mind when the Elder pictured the Spirit as "unction" (I John 2:20). As flame both creates and destroys, so the Spirit is called "fire" (Luke 3:16). Here the reference is to the Spirit's work in destroying evil and creating good.

He who hopes to speak of God faces a dilemma. He can attempt to use precise language, which is almost unintelligible except to a theologian. Or he can use picture language, which is intelligible but not precise. The technical language of theology is indeed grim and forbidding to the uninstructed. In that tongue, the Spirit is said to be "omniscient, omnipotent, and omnipresent." The inspired writers of Scripture faced the dilemma squarely and decided in favor of poetic, picturesque, imaginative language. Perhaps the most glorious passage concerning the Spirit in the entire Bible is the 139th Psalm. Note how it is packed with metaphors, all of which refer to the indescribable mystery of God's Spirit.

Whither shall I go from thy SPIRIT?
 or whither shall I flee from thy PRESENCE?
If I ascend up into heaven, thou art there:
 if I make my bed in hell, behold, thou art there.
If I take the wings of the morning,
 and dwell in the uttermost parts of the sea;
Even there shall thy HAND lead me,
 and thy RIGHT HAND shall hold me.

If I say, Surely the darkness shall cover me;
 even the night shall be LIGHT about me.
Yea, the darkness hideth not from thee;
  but the night shineth as the day:
  the darkness and the light are both alike to thee.
For thou hast possessed my reins:
  thou hast covered me in my mother's womb.
I will praise thee; for I am fearfully and wonder-
    fully made:
  marvellous are thy works; and that my soul
    knoweth right well.
My substance was not hid from thee, when I was
    made in secret,
  and curiously wrought in the lowest parts of the
    earth.
Thine EYES did see my substance, yet being
    unperfect;
  and in thy BOOK all my members were written,
  which in continuance were fashioned, when as
    yet there was none of them.
How precious also are thy THOUGHTS unto
    me, O God!
  how great is the sum of them!
If I should count them, they are more in number
    than the sand:
  when I awake, I am still with thee.

Psalm 139:7-18

I have emphasized only the nouns. There are at least
as many verbs in the quotation that might be emphasized. I trust it is clear that the Holy Spirit who inspired
the Scripture, favors the imaginative phrase, "The
darkness and the light are both alike to thee" in

preference to a technical term like "the omniscience of God."

Back to Middletown

In Middletown we have seen much that is good, and much that falls far short of being good. It is the church's elementary duty to foster and develop the good, and so doing to overcome the evil. In this task the church is not alone; for the Spirit of God fills the church, guides its members into the knowledge of God's will, and empowers them to do it. I have said that the outstanding need in the church today is to rediscover the Holy Spirit. This sounds as if God were lost, and man had to search for Him. The facts are just the opposite. Man is lost. God is searching for you. Your task is to recognize the stirrings of life within yourself, and to clear away the barriers to your spiritual development.

Rediscovering the Holy Spirit means far more than dusting off some theological formulae about the third Person of the Holy Trinity. These formulae came into being to give expression, as precise as possible, to soul-shaking experience our fathers had. Sometimes the language that meant much to one generation means little to another. So I am not especially interested in recapturing the religious vocabulary of yesterday. But I am praying instead that the church in our time may have anew the flaming consciousness that God is present, the intense concern for our neighbors, the confidence of God's guidance, the wholehearted commitment to God's will, and the peace of heart that are implied in the phrase, "I believe in the Holy Ghost."

2

THE SPIRIT AND THE BIBLE

The law of the Lord is perfect, converting
the soul: The testimony of the Lord is
sure, making wise the simple. The statutes
of the Lord are right, rejoicing the heart:
The commandment of the Lord is pure,
enlightening the eyes. The fear of the
Lord is clean, enduring for ever: The
judgments of the Lord are true and righteous
altogether. More to be desired are they
than gold, yea, than much fine gold: Sweeter
also than honey and the honeycomb.
Moreover by them is thy servant warned: And
in keeping of them there is great reward.

PSALM 19:7-11

All Christians agree that in some sense the Bible is inspired. The verb "inspire" means literally "breathe in." It suggests that the Holy Spirit has "breathed" life into the Scripture as once He breathed into man the breath of life when man became a living soul. The word "inspiration" is found only once within the Bible. "All scripture is given by inspiration of God" (II Timothy 3:16). Another Biblical term describing the sacred mystery is "revelation," literally, "taking away a

25

veil." It matters little which of these picturesque terms one uses. What matters is the response you make with your life to God's disclosure of His nature and purpose within the pages of the Book.

Some think it offensive that the basic knowledge of God should be found in a book. They would prefer that it be found in immediate mystical experience, or, the complete opposite, as the end link in a long chain of logical speculation. Most philosophic religions assume that final reality is to be found in one of these two ways, by losing contact with history either in contemplation or in mystical rapture. Christianity, by contrast, pinpoints the dates of God's redemptive activity in history. "The year that King Uzziah died. . . ." "In the fifteenth year of the reign of Tiberius Caesar, Pontius Pilate being governor of Judaea, and Herod being tetrarch of Galilee. . . ." "The third day he rose again from the dead. . . ." "When the day of Pentecost was fully come. . . ." If God has revealed Himself in history, then history must be recorded.

The Spirit and the Writer

The overwhelming majority of evangelical Christians today believe that the Spirit of God dealt with the writers of Holy Scripture, not in any mechanical way, but in complete harmony with the laws of their own inner being. He met them as they were, poets, sharecroppers, millionaires, fishermen, philosophers, and store clerks. Each human author of the Bible had his own cultural background, reflected in his distinctive vocabulary and style of writing. Each had a genetic makeup that set him apart from every other individual

in the world. Each lived on earth during a definite
historical period that colored his thoughts and actions.
There is no problem in accounting for the glorious
diversity of the Bible. Different kinds of people wrote
it, over a period of many centuries. Before the time of
writing, parts were handed down by oral tradition, for
how many years nobody can guess. The problem is the
unity, not the diversity, of the Bible. How does a book,
compiled in what seems a haphazard way, present unity
of development and theme?

We who believe the Bible is inspired look to the
divine Author behind the human authors to explain
the unity of the Book. The Holy Spirit inflamed the
hearts of men, giving them intense concern about serious problems. Then the Holy Spirit, working usually
through "natural" channels, guided human minds
toward the solutions. As Luke tells us, the historian
had to look up his references. The poets of the Bible,
like poets today, doubtless had to pace the floor, biting
their fingernails, while searching for the word that
would express a meaning with precision. But in all
their writings is more than the honest search for clarity
and beauty. The Biblical writers themselves believed
that God had "showed" (e.g., Micah 6:8) or "spoken"
(Isaiah 46:11) His truth to human agents, who then
were under compulsion to express what God had committed to them. "The lion hath roared, who will
not fear? the Lord God hath spoken, who can but
prophesy?" (Amos 3:8).

As the Apostle Paul writes to the church in Corinth
about the always-complex subject of marriage, he gives
us an indirect glimpse into the whole process of inspiration. In I Corinthians 7 he is writing about

marriage, to a congregation that faces persecution for the faith. And he shows a picture of one who has received a message from God, and believes that he is obligated to express that message with his own best thought. He says:

Unto the married I command, yet not I, but the Lord, Let not the wife. . . . (verse 10)

But to the rest speak I, not the Lord: If any brother. . . . (verse 12)

Now concerning virgins I have no commandment of the Lord: yet I give my judgment, as one that hath obtained mercy of the Lord. . . . (verse 25)

She is happier if she so abide, after my judgment: and I think also that I have the Spirit of God. (verse 40)

Some devout Christians believe that while the Bible was being written the human authors were in complete mental repose, contributing nothing to the content of the message. The Holy Spirit dictated it all, they were just stenographers. There are grave objections to this idea of mechanical inspiration. For one thing, Isaiah and Jeremiah just do not write the same kind of language. Each has a literary style of profound majesty, but they are quite different styles. The tight-knit, analytical reasoning in the epistle to the Hebrews is a world apart from the explosive, passionate outbursts of the Revelation. The first objection is the diversity that fills the Bible. But far more serious, the idea of mechanical inspiration misrepresents the Holy Spirit. As we know Him, the Holy Spirit is the indwelling God. Yet this viewpoint of mechanical inspiration shows the Spirit descending to mere external manipulation of people, in producing one of His most important works on earth.

There are many today who will agree that the Bible is inspired, and then proceed to define all meaning out of inspiration. To them it seems no more than a general religious feeling within the writers. This viewpoint is certainly easy to accept. It offers no difficulties whatsoever, but unfortunately it offers no voice of the living God either. In twentieth century jargon, "inspired" means "uplifting." I fear that many speak of the inspired Scripture in just such a way.

This easygoing attitude toward inspiration underlies a current popular heresy, the philosophy of religious syncretism. This means selecting the best from the world's religions. No one will deny that there is much of tremendous value in the religious writings of Confucius, Mohammed, and Gautama Buddha, for example. Their work is filled with religious exaltation, and keen analysis of human motive and conduct. So why not pick and choose the best from each religion and end with a satisfying super-religion?

The suggestion has a charm all its own, but it skips lightly over a basic issue, that of truth. No matter how satisfying a religious faith may seem, if it is not true one cannot long remain satisfied with it. Christians believe that the Bible is God's inspired Word to man. We believe that this Word offers a true picture of God's nature and of human destiny. We believe that it is God's message to us, not merely a record of our groping for Him. We find many points of agreement with other religions. These do not pose any special problems. But what of the disagreements? If one accepts the Bible as God's message, then one had better be very slow to improve upon it.

Those who believe that the Bible is inspired admit — nay we insist — that it is a thoroughly human document. It is a product of human minds, earthly cultures, historically conditioned attitudes, and all the rest that goes with the mortal quest for light. But it is more than this. Through these human agencies, God has brought a message to the world.

We cannot divide Scripture into two parts, the one divine and the other human. It is just as impossible to say where in Scripture the human ends and the divine begins or *vice versa,* as it is to tell where in man the body ends and the soul begins. The two interpenetrate, and as a result of this interpenetration the Bible is in its entirety, on the one hand, a human production, and on the other, a divine production.

> Louis Berkhof,
> *Manual of Reformed Doctrine,*
> Wm. B. Eerdmans Publishing Co.,
> p. 45

The Spirit and the Compilation

Today we take for granted that there is a Bible. It has been in existence for nigh two thousand years. For most of that period it has been a best seller. Yet the word "bible" means "the books." A cursory examination of the Bible will show that it contains sixty-six different books. Each of these sixty-six had to be written. And after that came a long period during which men must decide: Is this particular work rightly a part of the Scripture? Just as significantly and just as invisibly as He guided the writers, the Holy Spirit guided those who compiled the Bible.

In reading the Old Testament, you can find occasional mention of books such as *Jashar,* or *The Book of the Acts of Solomon,* or *The Book of the Chronicles of the Kings of Judah.* These were valuable works, dealing with religious subject matter. But they are not included in the Bible. Before acceptance as Scripture, each candidate for inclusion underwent a long process of testing, and these did not pass. For each book that finally was accepted, doubtless thousands were rejected. Gradually, over the centuries, a concensus developed within the community of faith. Humanly speaking, the agreement was a tribute to the inherent power of certain books. The Holy Spirit was working through the agency of human judgment.

From a tragedy in the fifth century before Christ we can learn something about the historical development of the Old Testament. In 432 B.C. the Samaritans split apart from the Jews, and built a temple on Mt. Gerizim. They held sacred only the first five books of our Bible, "The Law." Since the Samaritans considered themselves the truly orthodox, we infer that in 432 only five books were accepted by the entire Jewish community as God's Word.

By the year 180 B.C. the basic divisions of our Old Testament apparently were well determined. At least there is a quotation from Jesus, the son of Sirach, that the scholars have dated, in which he speaks of "The Law," "The Prophets," and "The Writings." These are the divisions still accepted by the Hebrews. Jesus of Nazareth acknowledged what we call the Old Testament as God's inspired Word. But after His time there still were rumblings of doubt within the Hebrew community, particularly concerning the books of Esther, Ecclesiastes, and the Song of Songs.

Along with the Old Testament had grown up a tremendous volume of valuable literary material; books like *Esdras, Tobit,* and *The Maccabees.* These were frequently circulated with the Scripture; for they are helpful religious reading. But they never were accepted as part of the Hebrew Scripture. Jerome, who translated the Bible into Latin in the fourth century, called these books "The Apocrypha," that is, "The Books of Hidden Wisdom." What we Protestants call "The Old Testament" he declared "canonical." What he called "The Apocrypha," he also declared to be "deutero-canonical." Unhappily the medieval church lost sight of the distinction. We Protestants have gone back to the early tradition. We recommend the Apocrypha as instructive reading, but we do not call it God's holy Word.

The chief significant difference made by our omitting what never was part of the Bible is the doctrine of purgatory, masses for the dead, and kindred beliefs. In II Maccabees 12:43, one finds that Judas Maccabeus sent "2000 drachmas of silver to Jerusalem for sacrifice, to be offered for the sins" of the dead. Upon this foundation the medieval church built the vast edifice of purgatory, and buttressed it with a couple of enigmatic verses from the New Testament. Without for a moment questioning that Judas Maccabeus believed in sacrifice for the sins of the dead, one may point out that Jesus Christ and His apostles said nothing about the matter that anyone thought worth recording.

In the earliest days the church had no written "New Testament." The apostles themselves formed a living link with Christ. From time to time, the apostles wrote letters to the churches, and many of these, quite naturally, were cherished by the recipients. As the original disciples of our Lord were put to death, one by one, Mark wrote his inspired biography of Jesus, to recapture in written form Simon Peter's recollection of the Savior. In the course of time the other Gospels followed. Yet still there was no written "New Testament." To us, the word "testament" denotes a particular book. More properly speaking, the testament is God's solemn compact with man, ratified upon a cross. The book is the record of that compact.

After the last sentence of the New Testament had been completed, there still was no "New Testament," as we call it. The books must be collected and credited with authority. Many and deep were the disagreements within the early Christian community, just as the Jewish fathers had disagreed. Again the Holy Spirit guided men in the selection of the right books. There was a tremendous volume of Christian literature, then as now, of widely varying merit. Luke mentions the many biographies of Jesus in his time from which he gathered the material for his work. In addition to the letters of Peter, Paul, James, and John that exist today, there must have been hundreds that have disappeared. Apollos, Priscilla, Aquila, Barnabas, Silas and the rest doubtless wrote. Others than John saw visions that they recorded. There would be a collection of Christian writings in this church, and quite a different collection in that church, and still another in the third church.

To the early Christians "The Scripture" meant our
Old Testament, but gradually the recognition grew
that the New Testament also is God's Word. In the
second century, Marcion, a business man of Asia
Minor, developed some strange and short-lived ideas
about Christianity. He decided that the God of the
Old Testament and the heavenly Father proclaimed
by Jesus were two separate Beings. So he organized a
Bible to prove it. He threw away the entire Old Testament, and incorporated only Luke's Gospel and ten of
Paul's letters into the New. Of course, he included a
book he had written himself. This is the first known
attempt to formulate the canon of the New Testament.
Happily, it did not succeed.

Along with the Marcionites were many other splinter
sects among the early Christians. (Christians have no
monopoly on divisiveness, but it is scarcely to our
credit that we so often succumb to a universal human
temptation.) To combat the sectarians, earnest Christians were forced to decide just which books constituted
the teaching of Christ and the apostles. By the end of
the second century, they had drawn the broad outlines
of the New Testament. But it required another two
centuries to decide finally about the more controversial
books. Eastern churches accepted Hebrews. In the early
days, the western churches rejected that spiritual masterpiece. With the Revelation, the contrary was the
case. The first record we have listing the twenty-seven
books of our New Testament was written by Athanasius
in 367. This was not confirmed by a church council
until 393.

The process of collection carried with it the process
of rejection. You read advertisements in the back of

cheap magazines about "the lost books of the Bible." These books were never lost; they were just passed over. Some early manuscripts of the New Testament contain one or more of them: *Clement of Rome, The Shepherd of Hermas, The Epistle of Barnabas,* and others. Since these are included in New Testament manuscripts, one must conclude that someone thought them parts of the New Testament. In reading these books you will find some that is cheap and tawdry, along with much that is pure and fine. But the spiritual flame that crackles through the New Testament is missing. The pages of our New Testament blaze. At their best, the "lost" books merely glow. In addition to these honest works of faith were some deliberate forgeries, such as *The Gospel according to Pontius Pilate.*

The Holy Scripture is marked with no external credentials that acclaim it the Word of God. Devout, intelligent Christians have differed vigorously about the parts that should comprise the Bible. But the Spirit led them to a conclusion. Today we have the Bible. Almost two centuries ago, Voltaire is reported to have said that in another hundred years the Bible would be but a historic relic. Perhaps by coincidence, the house where he was living at the time is now headquarters of a Bible Society. The Bible has demonstrated a strange power of endurance. Our fathers who selected the books comprising the Bible chose well. But the final result is not merely human. The strong Hand of God guided the selection of the books that He knew would be needed down through the ages of mankind.

In bringing about the selection of the books that comprise the Bible, the Holy Spirit worked through "natural" channels. People compared and contrasted

and chose what was best in preference to what was
merely good. The Holy Spirit did not override man's
judgment; He worked through it.

The Spirit and the Copyist

After the many hazards of compilation, the Holy
Scripture faced another grave danger, that of distortion
by the copyist. You can easily make an experiment that
will demonstrate the danger. Copy an extended piece
of prose. Copy it carefully, with full attention. Then
copy your copy, and repeat the process several times.
If your tenth copy is identical with the original, the
church really needed you about sixteen centuries ago.
Until Gutenberg developed the printing press, all
books were painstakingly copied by hand. As your
experiment has showed, even a careful copyist sometimes makes mistakes. That the Holy Bible survived
fifteen centuries of hand copying without serious error
being introduced is nothing short of a miracle.

Among the Hebrews was a professional corps of
copyists, to whom every Christian owes an incalculable
debt of gratitude. The scrolls they copied were intended for use, and in course of time they were worn out.
So it developed that until the quite recent past the
oldest Hebrew manuscript we had for the Old Testament dated from about the ninth century. Then in
1947, ancient scrolls were discovered near the Dead
Sea. Among these was the roll of Isaiah. Various
scholarly tests, including analysis for radio-active carbon, have given a date of approximately 100 B.C. for
this scroll. So at a single jump, we were a millennium
closer to the words that Isaiah actually wrote. And the
difference that had crept in during those thousand

years? Practically nothing. We have — in the case of Isaiah, and presumably the rest of the Old Testament — the selfsame Scripture that Jesus knew and loved, and respected as the Voice of God.

With the New Testament, there was no such happy arrangement during the earlier centuries. Most of the Christians were poor, and could not afford to hire the professional Roman copyists. So one of the brothers would volunteer to undertake copying as a work of piety. Sometimes he was not especially well equipped for the task. Occasionally he would leave out a line, sometimes he would copy a word twice; of course he would misspell words. Sometimes he would copy a note in the margin as part of the text. One student of the subject has said, "I cannot imagine a single mistake that the early copyists did not make in profusion." By the time the Christians had developed a tradition of careful, scholarly copying it took us centuries — the scribes painstakingly reproduced all the mistakes their predecessors carelessly had made.

The nineteenth century was an age of outstanding manuscript discovery. With "new" materials to study, scholars were able to draw closer and closer to the actual words written down by Matthew, Mark, and the rest. One finding of these scholars has deeply disturbed many Christians. They point out that today there are 250,000 variant readings for the New Testament. For a volume containing less than 200,000 words, this would seem a considerable achievement. Where does the Holy Spirit fit into this picture? Evidently not in keeping men from any variance, but rather in keeping them from serious error.

Look at the variations. Ninety per cent of them are mistakes in spelling, or minor changes in the word order, the presence or absence of "the," and matters of equal gravity. Of the remainder, 95 per cent do not matter. A typical example is found in the incident of the Syrophenician woman, as recorded by Mark. The majority of manuscripts read, "Yes, Lord. . . ." However, the Codex Bezae, a magnificent Latin-Greek uncial manuscript from the sixth century, reads, "But, Lord. . . ." The Codex Borgianus, an Egyptian-Greek manuscript from the fifth century, reads simply "Lord. . . ." It is the task of Biblical scholars to weigh the value of the different texts, and to decide which of these three readings represents what Mark wrote. Here, as in most places, truth lies in small distinctions. Whichever reading may finally be accepted, we who are not students of ancient manuscripts may still correctly understand our Savior's mercy to an alien woman.

Now we are down to the manuscript variations that make a difference:

Did Jesus include at the end of the Lord's Prayer the words: "For thine is the kingdom and the power and the glory, for ever. Amen"? The manuscript evidence is that He did not.

Which, if any, of three disputed endings to Mark's Gospel did Mark write? Probably none of them. Mark's ending is lost.

Did Luke say "Good will to men" or "to men of good will"? A letter "s" makes all that difference. Probably Luke said, "men of good will."

Did John include the section about the woman taken

in adultery that now appears in John 8:1-11? The manuscript evidence is that he did not.

Was the Trinitarian formula in I John 5:7 part of the original manuscript? Apparently not.

These variations, it seems to me, are about the most significant to be found in New Testament manuscript study. I culled them from Westcott and Hort's edition of the Greek New Testament, a masterpiece of reverent scholarship. In this masterpiece is a brief note about the textual criticism of the Bible, which might profitably be read by all who fear that scholarly investigation can weaken Christian faith:

> This brief account of the text of the New Testament would be incomplete without a word of caution against a natural misunderstanding. Since textual criticism has various readings for its subject, and the discrimination of genuine readings from corruptions for its aim, discussions on textual criticism almost inevitably obscure the simple fact that variations are but secondary incidents' of a fundamentally single and identical text. In the New Testament in particular it is difficult to escape an exaggerated impression as to the proportion which the words subject to variation bear to the whole text, and also, in most cases, as to their intrinsic importance. It is not superfluous therefore to state explicitly that the great bulk of the words of the New Testament stand out above all discriminative processes of criticism, because they are free from variation. . . . If comparative trivialities, such as changes of order, the insertion or omission of the article with proper names, and the

like, are set aside, the words in our opinion still subject to doubt can hardly amount to more than a thousandth part of the whole New Testament.

p. 564

No basic doctrine of Christianity rests upon a disputed passage of Scripture. We may not always have the precise word that Luke or John wrote. A century of manuscript examination is underlining the conclusion, we have a reliable record of their thought. Once it was the fashion to explain away every difficult problem in the Bible as an "interpolation." The fashion has pretty well died out, for lack of support by manuscript evidence.

As you hold your Bible in your hand, you can thank the Holy Spirit of God, first, for guiding the men who wrote it, then for guiding the men who selected some parts and rejected other contenders, and then for guiding those who copied. In another place we shall look at His activity in the lives of those who translated the Scripture. Hold the Book reverently. It is a miracle. It is one of God's outstanding works on earth. Like much of the Spirit's work, it was carried out by men.

The Spirit and the Reader

"I hear you *say* it's the Word of God, but how can I *know* it's the Word of God?" You will not speak often of the Bible without having the question asked you. And it is a perfectly fair question. I am afraid that the only possible answer will be at first unsatisfactory to those who ask. Theirs is the age-old demand for proof. The Pharisees asked Jesus, "Give us a sign." And Jesus refused, because a "sign" would be irrelevant. Some truths are too big to be proved.

So it is with the Holy Bible. After you have assembled the rational arguments to prove it the Word of God, you still have not proved your case. You have assembled arguments about which people can argue forever. In the meantime, other people are reading the Bible and discovering, each in his own way: "This is God's Word to me." The final step of inspiration comes when the Holy Spirit assures you that the message in your hand comes from headquarters. When people by the hundred million, from every natural and cultural climate, come independently to this same conclusion, their opinion should be treated with considerable respect, even though one has not yet accepted it himself.

They who have been inwardly taught by the Spirit, feel an entire acquiescence in the Scripture. . . . It is self-authenticated, carrying with it its own evidence, and ought not to be made the subject of demonstration and arguments from reason; but it obtains the credit which it deserves with us by the testimony of the Spirit. For though it conciliate our reverence by its internal majesty, it never seriously affects us till it is confirmed by the Spirit in our hearts. Therefore, being illuminated by him, we now believe the divine original of the Scripture.

John Calvin,
Institutes, I, vii, 5

Perhaps a comparison will help in regard to the truth demonstrated by reason and that demonstrated by faith. There follow two statements, both true. (1) The earth is 93,000,000 miles from the sun. (2) A person ought to keep his promises. The first is proved by reason. If you know how, and if you have the equipment, you can prove it to anyone who has the ability to follow you. But what of the second? Though it is a matter of daily experience, and of far more practical importance, you do not demand that it be proved. You are simply, directly, immediately aware that it is true. Attempt to prove it. You will come up with something like, "Suppose nobody kept his promises, what would follow?" Then you could reel off a long list of disastrous consequences, all perfectly true, and all irrelevant. You were sure of the conclusion before you began the argument. Be your arguing good or bad, it is pointless. The psychologist would describe one's knowledge of a moral duty as "intuition." The Christian would describe it further as the voice of the Holy Spirit.

How can I know that the Bible is the Word of God? If you wait for me to argue you into believing it, you will wait forever. But there is one way you can find out. Read the Bible, and let the Holy Spirit tell you.

3

THE SPIRIT OF THE CHURCH

Now there are diversities of gifts, but the same Spirit. And there are differences of administrations, but the same Lord. And there are diversities of operations, but it is the same God which worketh all in all. But the manifestation of the Spirit is given to every man to profit withal. For to one is given by the Spirit the word of wisdom, to another the word of knowledge by the same Spirit; to another faith by the same Spirit; to another the gifts of healing by the same Spirit; to another the working of miracles; to another prophecy; to another discerning of spirits; to another divers kinds of tongues; to another the interpretation of tongues: but all these worketh that one and the selfsame Spirit, dividing to every man severally as he will. For as the body is one, and hath many members, and all the members of that one body, being many, are one body: so also is Christ. For by one Spirit are we all baptized into one body, whether we be Jews or Gentiles, whether we be bond or free; and have been all made to drink into one Spirit. For the body is not one member, but many. If the foot shall say, Because I am not the hand, I am not of the body; is it therefore not of the body? And if the ear shall say, Because I am not the eye, I am not of the body; is it therefore not of the body? If the whole body were an eye, where were the hearing? If the whole were hearing, where were the smelling? But now hath God set the members every one of them in the body, as it hath pleased him. And if they were all one member, where were the body? But now are they many members, yet but one body. And the eye cannot say unto the hand, I have no need of thee: nor again the head to the feet, I have no need of you. Nay, much more those members of the body, which seem to be more feeble, are necessary: And those members of the body, which we think to be less honourable, upon these we bestow more abundant honour; and our uncomely parts have more abundant comeliness. For our comely parts have no need: but God hath tempered the body together, having given more abundant honour to that part which lacked: That there should be no schism in the body; but that the members should have the same care one for another. And whether one member suffer, all the members suffer with it; or one member be honoured, all the members rejoice with it. Now ye are the body of Christ, and members in particular. And God hath set some in the church, first apostles, secondarily prophets, thirdly teachers, after that miracles, then gifts of healings, helps, governments, diversities of tongues. Are all

apostles? are all prophets? are all teachers? are all
    workers of miracles? Have all the gifts of
      healing? do all speak with tongues? do all
    interpret? But covet earnestly the best gifts: and
    yet shew I unto you a more excellent way.

I CORINTHIANS 12:4-31

So important is the thirteenth chapter of First Corinthians that Christians sometimes overlook the humbler, but still important, chapter that precedes. In the thirteenth chapter, the Apostle writes about the duty of every Christian everywhere, to reflect the love of Christ in his daily life. Underlying the general duty, each Christian has his own specific duties. As individually we Christians do our work, the general health of the church results. The Apostle is careful to point out that this health is no accident, or even a product of human design. This is the way the Holy Spirit operates.

The Spirit of Variety

If the well-known man from Mars had visited the church in ancient Corinth, doubtless he would have spent considerable time trying to understand its apparently diverse activities. The church in Corinth was concerned that its members have enough to eat. The members were committed to worship together. They shared with one another their most intense sorrows. They united in joy. Birth, marriage, death — the church cared deeply about all these pivotal events in life. This member of the church was a scholar. That member was a doctor. Another was an interpreter. This member had her hands more than full with the problem of raising a family. Another member worked down at the waterfront, wrestling heavy bales of merchandise onto the ships. Yet these people, so different in their appearance and function, were bound together into a unity. The church in Corinth was concerned, not about this or that aspect of the human personality, but about the total person in his relationship with God. This concern had many different expressions.

One of the members might have showed the visitor a letter from Paul, cherished in the church archives, in which the Apostle said about this variety that is the church:

There are diversities of gifts, but the same Spirit. And there are differences of administrations, but the same Lord. And there are diversities of operations, but it is the same God which worketh all in all.

If the visitor from Mars came to the church in Middletown, he would find much different, much the same. Language and costumes would be different, of course. The church would be housed in a far better building. The members would earn their living in ways unimagined nineteen centuries ago. But he would find the same concern about the total personality, being expressed in an even greater number of ways.

Here, for example, is a group of dedicated men and women, who may earn their daily bread as airplane mechanics, typists, housewives, analogue computer operators, and insurance adjusters. Only the housewife today had any recognizable counterpart in ancient Corinth. Yet these devout people engage, week after week, in the selfsame work of teaching that was so

important in the Corinthian church. Though they
have better materials to work with, the faith they
proclaim is unchanged.

The church in our time is so vast and complex that
we have need for much administration. As everyone
knows who has endured many committee meetings, not
all have been blessed with the gift of leadership. Some
people have the ability to get things done. Others,
apparently, do not. Every clergyman I know deplores
the amount of time and energy that he must give to
the routine work of keeping the church machinery
oiled and in relatively frictionless operation. The pastor in Middletown daily thanks his Creator for the
devoted, loyal church members who give their talents
freely in the work of church administration. The pastor
cannot do one tenth of the organizational work that
must be done. But the work is done, because loyal
volunteers do it.

A group of high school students gathers in the
church office every Thursday afternoon to fold papers
and stuff envelopes and perform a hundred other
unexciting, but necessary, chores.

One member explained to the pastor, "I can't make
a large pledge right now. But I can give some time.
I'm a licensed electrician. If there's any electrical work
that needs installing or fixing, let me know." Just to
be on the safe side, the electrician inspects his church
regularly. He said to a neighbor, "This is God's house.
It's my job to see that it's properly wired."

A committee of devoted men and women regularly
visit with the sick and feeble. Another committee calls
on all the newcomers in the neighborhood. Another

group is studying the work of the church in Africa. Another group is sewing for the leper hospital.

Unless he made a really extended visit, the visitor from Mars would not see, or even imagine, the most important group of all. Respectfully, the other church members call these people "The Powerhouse." More formally, they are entitled "The Guild of Intercessors." Sometimes they refer to themselves as "The Wheelchair Brigade." They are the shut-ins, who cannot give their physical energy to serve their Lord through His church. Instead they give their prayers. While others sometimes are so busy doing good that they forget why they are working so feverishly, these Intercessors remember daily that the church is a visible expression of Christ's Spirit on earth. Daily they seek, and find, God's blessing upon the work He is doing through His children, the members of the visible church.

There are many different ways of serving God within His church. Not everybody has the necessary ability to serve Him in each of these ways. Here, for example, is a young woman who has a wonderful contralto voice. Her checkbook, however, is a perpetual mess. Her neighbor is an accountant. Yet we must say, in all charity, that when he tries to sing he makes noises like a wounded duck. There is important work in the church for each of them. Obviously it is not the same work. One can help others to worship in the beauty of holiness. The other can see to it that the church's finances are handled with integrity, without the scandalous laxity that some Protestants have demonstrated in their fiscal affairs.

Differing people have differing abilities. You are

responsible to use your abilities to the glory of your
Father in heaven. You are not responsible to praise
God with your neighbor's gifts. That is your neighbor's
task. He who is repairing a short circuit, she who is
stuffing envelopes, he who is balancing the accounts,
she who is singing in the choir, he who is organizing
the budget committee, she who prays for hours each
day from her wheel-chair — these saints whose work
for Christ is so different, all are serving Him.

Christian service cannot stop short at the perform-
ance of one particular task, no matter how well it be
performed. Every Christian is required to express his
faith in love, all the time. Undergirding this, each
particular Christian must put his own special talents
to work for the Savior. The Holy Spirit has given many
different abilities. Many are needed within the church.

The Spirit of Unity

There was a serious problem within the church of
Corinth. Unhappily, there are traces of the same problem in the Middletown church. In ancient Corinth a
church member might become so intensely concerned
about his Christian work that he would disparage the
work his Christian brother was doing. So in Middletown are those who appear to think that everything
should move over for the choir, and those who would
willingly close down all activities except the Boy
Scouts, and those who think the church year has been
a success if only the budget is balanced. Each is rightly
concerned about the importance of his own service.
Each is tempted to forget the unity to which his work
must contribute.

To describe the unity that is the church, the Apostle Paul introduces the beautiful expression "the body of Christ." This concept of the body, as a group of people gathered together for a common purpose, has become a pivotal idea in our civilization. Today we use the Latin form "corporation" to express this idea. The corporation, legally speaking, is a fictitious personality, by means of which many persons can act as one. In the Biblical concept there is no fiction whatsoever. As the eternal Christ walked on earth long ago in a human body, today He walks and talks on earth through His body, the church.

A body consists of many members. Hands, feet, eyes, ears — these are members of the human body. Contraltos, invalids, accountants, teachers — these are members of Christ's earthly body. The world has borrowed the idea of membership from the church, and considerably changed its meaning in the process.

Without really thinking about it, a person will say, "I am a member of the Chowder and Marching Society." If you press him to explain, he will say, "I *belong* to the club." Does he? In what meaningful sense does he *belong* to this worthwhile organization? He has voluntarily associated himself with a group of like-minded people, who enjoy eating chowder and marching about. He pays his dues and attends most of the meetings. In modern English, this means he is a member of the Society. Unhappily, many seem to think that church membership implies no more. Remembering that Jesus' hands once were pierced with nails, we dare not think that membership in His body will always be pleasant and painless.

To a Christian, membership in the body of Christ means the final loyalty of his life. To the world, membership means a fairly loose attachment to an organization. Earthly laws cannot well distinguish between those organizations to which people attach themselves, and that body into which the Holy Spirit draws those who are redeemed. The distinction is one the Christian must make himself. He really belongs to the body of Christ. He may well be associated with a dozen other worthwhile societies, but he does not literally belong to them. He has already given his ultimate allegiance to Christ, who has redeemed him. "Ye are not your own; for ye are bought with a price: therefore glorify God in your body, and in your spirit, which are God's" (I Corinthians 6:19-20).

A person does not lose his individuality through belonging to the body of Christ. It is the disciples of Satan who lose their identity, not the disciples of Jesus. A man going to the devil in Middletown today follows the same well-trodden primrose path that led to the devil in ancient Babylon. There is remarkably little to choose between the cruelties of Adolph Hitler and those of Tiglath Pileser. Evil has a dull, horrible, monotonous, ugly sameness, wherever you find it. Good offers the sparkle of variety. It is the saints who differ from one another, not the sinners. The saints have found their true individuality by becoming part of a unity that is greater than self. They are members of Christ's earthly body.

Once the eternal Christ walked on earth in a human body. He had need for food, clothing, shelter, and all the other material requirements of human existence.

His body endured fatigue, hunger, cold, and exposure. When Jesus said, "the flesh is weak," He spoke from experience. Yet this weak body, which finally bled to death, served for years as the instrument of His eternal will. Today the church on earth is the visible body of Christ. The members are His hands, His eyes, His feet. God knows how weak these members are; still He has chosen them to be the agents of His eternal will on earth.

The Spirit of Harmony

A body consists of many interdependent members. Its health depends largely upon the proper functioning of each. The members of the church, who have been called into the unity of faith, have many different talents. Each is expected to contribute what he can best give in his Lord's service. Each should respect what his Christian brother is able to do. Some of the Christians in Corinth forgot this. Some were so obsessed with the importance of their own work that they looked down on their neighbors' contribution. And others were so bashful about their ability that they decided to do nothing. The Apostle chided both with gentle humor:

If the foot shall say, Because I am not the hand, I am not of the body; is it therefore not of the body? And if the ear shall say, Because I am not the eye, I am not of the body; is it therefore not of the body? If the whole body were an eye, where were the hearing? If the whole were hearing, where were the smelling? But now hath God set the members every one of them in the body, as it hath pleased him.

No individual has the ability to do all that is needed within the church. No Christian is so lacking in ability that he can do nothing at all. A person's native ability may be so small that his contribution seems trivial to some. Let none despise it. If he is giving his best, he is contributing to the health of Christ's earthly body. Another may have so many abilities that he is tempted to think of himself more highly than he ought. The Holy Spirit, speaking through the Apostle Paul, urges each member of Christ's body to remember that he has an important function, and to remember at the same time that there are other important functions.

Within the human body we emphasize the importance of certain organs, and slight the importance of others. Quite obviously a person can go through life without a little toe much better than he could without a thumb. Of course some work within the church of Christ is more significant than some other. The church can exist without mimeograph machines, but the church could not long exist without teachers. Yet the one who does the humble, routine (and messy) work of operating the mimeograph machine is making her contribution to the church — if that is the best she can offer — just as truly as the one who teaches.

When I was young it was practically the standard procedure to remove a child's tonsils at the earliest possible moment. Not long ago I was talking with a doctor about a young friend of ours whose throat was badly infected. I was somewhat surprised to hear him saying, "I'm going to save those tonsils if it's humanly possible." Doctors have evidently decided that these uncomely parts serve a purpose, that God has tempered the body together. So it is with the church.

No human body is completely healthy. I am sure that Jesus, in the days of His flesh, knew sickness, as one member or another of His body was ill. Just so, the body of Christ on earth today is not completely healthy. Many people enjoy telling me what is wrong with the church, how the members fail to live fully Christian lives, and so forth. I always listen as politely as I can. But at the back of my mind is a wistful longing that I could return to my days of innocence when I knew as little about the faults of the church as do its critics. One who works within the church learns quite rapidly that the body of Christ is not in perfect health. Yet this body, despite the weakness of its individual members, is growing. Growth is a sign of life. It indicates that the forces of health are stronger than the forces of sickness.

The Holy Spirit has drawn into a fellowship people of all kinds and varieties. If you want to look at them negatively, God knows there are faults aplenty to be seen. In his work *General William Booth Enters Into Heaven,* the poet Vachel Lindsay has imaginatively depicted these, the uncomely and infirm members of Christ's body.

Booth led boldly with his big bass drum —
(Are you washed in the blood of the Lamb?)
The Saints smiled gravely and they said: "He's come."
(Are you washed in the blood of the Lamb?)

Walking lepers followed, rank on rank,
Lurching bravoes from the ditches dank,
Drabs from the alleyways and drug fiends pale —
Minds still passion-ridden, soul powers frail: —
Vermin-eaten saints with mouldy breath,
Unwashed legions with the ways of death —
(Are you washed in the blood of the Lamb?)

Are these members of Christ's body? Assuredly no
other corporation on earth would want them. Where
would they fit in General Motors? What could West-
inghouse do with them? What good are they to society
or to the church? The Christian, in his best moments,
does not ask such questions. He is not at first concerned to discover what the sinner can do for Christ,
but rather what Christ can do for the sinner. The
poet continues:

Jesus came from out the court-house door,
Stretched his hands above the passing poor.
Booth saw not, but led his queer ones there
Round and round the mighty court-house square.
Yet in an instant all that blear review
Marched on spotless, clad in raiment new.
The lame were straightened, withered limbs un-
    curled
And blind eyes opened on a new, sweet world.
Drabs and vixens in a flash made whole!
Gone was the weasel head, the snout, the jowl!
Sages and sybils now, and athletes clean,
Rulers of empires and of forests green!
The hosts were sandalled, and their wings were
    fire!
(Are you washed in the blood of the Lamb?)

But their noise played havoc with the angel-choir.
(Are you washed in the blood of the Lamb?)
Oh shout Salvation! It was good to see
Kings and Princes by the Lamb set free.

As one looks about the church, it is easy to find
faults. The congregation sings too loud. The preacher
is not practical enough. The ushers' shoes squeak. The
members, one and all, are not good enough to belong
to the body of Christ. Only a few members represent
society's failures. Most of them hold honorable posi-
tions in business, industry, and professions. But all
have fallen short of God's glory. None is really worthy
to be a church member. Yet the Holy Spirit has gathered together, from every caste and class, from every
race and color, from every land and tongue, the members of Christ's body, the church. Each has his own
talents and abilities. Much is expected from him who
has received much. Less is expected from him who
has received little. No Christian is so strong that he
can live without the aid of his fellow Christians. And
no Christian is so weak that he has nothing at all to
contribute to the health of his church.

The body of Christ today is filled with aches and
pains. All sorts of things are wrong with the church.
The sopranos flat, and the meetings are too long, and
the preacher does not talk loud enough. Dwell on these
faults if you will. Many do. But we who love the church
try to see beyond its present weaknesses and faults, to
behold "Kings and Princes by the Lamb set free." In
the meantime, the Holy Spirit works through the
church as it is. All sorts of different people, with all
sorts of different failings, and all sorts of different

abilities comprise the church. And the Holy Spirit has taught us to consider them members of the body of the living Christ, through whom God works on earth today.

4

THE SPIRIT IN SALVATION
The Primacy of Faith

And when they had laid many stripes upon them,
they cast them into prison, charging the
jailor to keep them safely: who, having received
such a charge, thrust them into the inner
prison, and made their feet fast in the stocks.
And at midnight Paul and Silas prayed, and
sang praises unto God: and the prisoners heard
them. And suddenly there was a great
earthquake, so that the foundations of the
prison were shaken: and immediately all the
doors were opened, and every one's bands
were loosed. And the keeper of the prison
awaking out of his sleep, and seeing the prison
doors open, he drew out his sword, and would
have killed himself, supposing that the prisoners
had been fled. But Paul cried with a loud
voice, saying, Do thyself no harm: for we are
all here. Then he called for a light, and
sprang in, and came trembling, and fell down
before Paul and Silas, and brought them
out, and said, Sirs, what must I do to be saved?
And they said, Believe on the Lord Jesus Christ,

and thou shalt be saved, and thy house. And
they spake unto him the word of the Lord,
and to all that were in his house. And he took
them the same hour of the night, and washed
their stripes; and was baptized, he and all his,
straightway. And when he had brought
them into his house, he set meat before them, and
rejoiced, believing in God with all his house.

ACTS 16:23-34

God's Message to You

One day I gave a test to some Sunday School students.
First I told them a story, then I asked them a single
question. The story is: You and a friend are thrown
into jail for the crime of being Christian. It has happened to thousands of people during the past few
years. You are horsewhipped and salt is rubbed into
the wounds. Your dungeon is slimy and dark, crawling
with bugs, and reeking with the smell of human sweat.
Every muscle in your body screams in agony. So you
and your friend begin to sing hymns to keep your
courage up. In the middle of the night there is an
earthquake. The prison warden comes running into
your cell, and he says, "Fellows, I'm scared. What can
I do to get over my fear?" The question is: "Suppose
all this happens to you, what do you tell the warden?"

I gave this test to a group of intelligent high school
age boys and girls. One of them said, "I'd tell him he
ought to attend church." Another said, "He ought to
learn how to pray." Another said, "I think that he
ought to read the Bible." Then, knowing my enthusi-
asm for the church, the Bible, and prayer, they all sat
and beamed and waited for me to beam back.

I did not beam. I suggested sadly that Jesus came into the world to set us free from the mistake they were making, that of thinking we can tug ourselves up to heaven by our own spiritual exercises. So I asked them to open their Bibles to Acts 16, and see how Paul and Silas, as guided by the Holy Spirit, handled a comparable situation. The students read in their Bibles, then one of them said, "You didn't get the question right. You were supposed to ask, 'What must I do to be saved?' but you asked, 'What must I do to get over my fear?' "

We know God's answer to the question, "What must I do to be saved?" The answer is, "Believe on the Lord Jesus Christ, and thou shalt be saved." That message is the key sentence of evangelical Christianity. The trouble with our answer is that nobody ever asks the question. But by the thousands and by the millions intelligent, thoughtful people are asking closely related questions.

"I'm losing my sight, and I'm scared. What'll I do?"

"My foreman picks on me all the time, and it's getting me down. What can I do about it?"

"I've started to drink and I can't stop. What can I do about it?"

"I always used to be so active. But now I'm cooped up in this wheel-chair, and I feel so useless. I'm beginning to wonder if there's a God at all. If there is, He doesn't care much about my feelings."

A pastor never goes through a week without hearing these and similar cries for help. In seeking for the answers, he must use every available resource of medi-

cine, law, social science, and the other valuable tools
of our culture. But he remembers that man is more
than a physical organism that can experience pain.
Every human problem is, at its heart, a spiritual problem. There can be no lasting solution to any human
problem if one ignores the central relationship of life,
that with almighty God. As far as I can remember,
nobody has ever asked me, in precisely these words,
"What must I do to be saved?" As people bring to me
their tangled personal problems, they never seem to
get the question right, but God's answer applies. Believe in the Lord Jesus Christ, and thou shalt be saved
from fear, from jealousy, from resentment, and all the
other demons that torture the modern soul. God's
answer has both an earthly and an eternal meaning.
The question, however it be phrased, usually arises
from a particular, troublesome, earthly problem.

Salvation and Struggle

When a person believes in the Lord Jesus Christ,
and so is saved, he has not come to the end of his
earthly struggles. There is a travesty of Christian faith
making the rounds today, to the general effect that, by
believing such and such, and doing such and such, you
can become pretty, popular, and successful. This is not
Christianity, it is black magic. After black magic has
been baptized, it is still bad. If you genuinely follow
Jesus, who died on a cross, you will scarcely be able to
avoid the normal hazards of human life. Jesus pointed
out that the rain falls on the just and the unjust. A
Christian's house can burn down as fast as a pagan's.
Being saved is no escape from the storm. It is strength
to man the oars when the going is rough.

Can you imagine what a hoax Christianity would be on any other basis? If belief in Christ brought good luck automatically, we would have millions of pious frauds in the world, instead of the dozens we have today. Christ promises no material gain in this stage of our existence. The aim of Christian faith is Christlike character, not wealth or prominence.

None of us has reached Christ's level of character. None of us deserves the unspeakable privilege of calling God his Father. None of us is worthy to be called a child of His. But the mystery and miracle of faith is, God accepts the beginning for the final result. When a person by faith becomes a Christian, he is adopted into the family of God, though his life — as yet — is far from being Christlike. At best he approaches the goal during earthly life. But we believe that what the Holy Spirit has begun in time He will complete in eternity.

We do not know, of course, all that was in the prison warden's mind when he asked, "What must I do to be saved?" He had been through the physical terror that comes to anyone in a time of danger. On top of that was the threat to his life, if any of the prisoners were to escape. He was at the point of suicide when Paul assured him, "Do thyself no harm; for we are all here." Of this we can be sure, the warden was a thoroughly shaken man, who was convinced that two of his prisoners had a spiritual security that he lacked; so he asked them how he could know this security. They told him, "Believe on the Lord Jesus Christ, and thou shalt be saved."

How can I learn to keep my temper?

Why am I always fighting with my mother-in-law?

What can I do about the worries that keep me awake all night?

When someone asks questions like these, it is scarcely helpful to advise him that a Christlike person would not be irritable, quarrelsome, or worried. He needs to learn how to become such a Christlike person. Down through the ages, the Holy Spirit has been helping those who are lost in the clouds of insecurity, anxiety, despair, and other varieties of sin. However the outward circumstances may differ, man's fundamental problem is the same as that of the Philippian jailor. He needs to enter into the right relationship with God. To each who is lost today, the Holy Spirit proclaims the same message, "Believe in the Lord Jesus Christ, and thou shalt be saved."

The Question of Priority

There are many in the world of our time who admire the moral teachings of Jesus, and honestly think that the church is making a big mistake in emphasizing faith instead of conduct. I have seen a creed that begins, "We believe in salvation by character." The evangelical Christian believes that the final goal of his life is to be a Christlike person. And he knows that faith is the direct road to that goal, not a detour. Code, creed, and cult are the outward aspects of Christianity that the world can see and appraise. Each has its place of tremendous importance. Each grows directly from a person's relationship with Christ. Yet it is idolatry to give any one of these vital emphases the place that belongs to Christ alone.

Nobody will deny the importance of Christian behavior. Many argue that this aspect of faith should receive the first emphasis in our teaching; then the relationship with Christ. For example; about eighty years ago Messrs. Moody and Sankey were making an evangelistic tour of Britain. Some of the respectable churchgoers were repelled by their insistence that man cannot save himself. A jingle appeared in *Punch* that expressed this feeling:

Declare not, O Moody, that doing is damning;
  And sing not, O Sankey, that working is sin;
For if piety be not emotional shamming
  Old duty's bedrock is the place to begin.

That, you recall, is precisely where my high school students were, eighty years later, laying all their emphasis upon man's effort to better himself, and calling it Christianity. Is it best to begin Christian faith by proclaiming the importance of action or the importance of Christ? The Holy Spirit evidently has decided it is best to begin with Christ.

Which comes first, the thought or the act? Most actions that are not the conscious outgrowth of thoughts are heedless, irresponsible, and destructive. The achievements that matter in this world almost all develop from seed thoughts that have borne fruit. The Golden Gate bridge, for example, was only a dream for years. But the dream would not vanish in daylight, and it began to take form as sketches and soundings and stress analyses. The bridge that you and I can see, and drive over, or sail under, is the realization of a thought. Could it be otherwise with Christianity? If we laid our stress upon the moral virtues, which all decent, civilized people accept, would this enable us

to develop Christlike character? Decent, civilized
people put Jesus to death.

The same person who derides the importance of a
good faith may emphasize the importance of a bad
faith. A burning question in our time is the proper
way to deal with intellectual Communists. A professor
of chemistry at an important university was a Communist. His students testified unanimously that he had
never, in any way, tried to influence their thoughts
about political matters. He was, further, an excellent
teacher of chemistry. The board of trustees in the university decreed that no one who holds to a vicious faith
should be entrusted with the delicate responsibility of
teaching. The American Association of University Professors held that a person must commit an evil act
before being condemned. The trustees countered that
a vicious faith will lead a person to commit, or at least
to condone, vicious actions. I am not debating the delicate question of constitutional law involved here. I am
just pointing out that many believe a bad faith produces bad results. Yet a member of this board of
trustees once said to me, "I don't care what a person's
religion is, as long as he is kind."

Suppose, for a fantastic moment, that Moody and
Sankey had toured England with a "gospel" to the
effect: "Be industrious. Be thrifty. Be sober." There
would have been loud applause after each impassioned
presentation. Then what? Everybody agrees that industry, thrift, and sobriety are admirable. But I know of
few indeed who have been argued into such virtue.
Instead Moody and Sankey chose God's message. "Believe in the Lord Jesus Christ, and thou shalt be saved."

And the sluggard who believed became industrious. The wastrel who believed became careful. The drunkard who believed became sober. On strictly practical grounds, God's message seems to produce Christian character far more quickly than any other approach.

When I was serving with the Navy, the doctors and the chaplains used to line up the sailors and give them long, terrifying lectures about the hazards to be encountered ashore in man's pursuit of happiness. As far as I could see, these lectures were largely a waste of educated breath. It is quite difficult to scare men into morality. I well recall one young sailor who lost his sight, drinking a concoction called Butterfly Rum. He explained to me, "I knew it was dangerous, but I hadn't had a drink in months." I recall several strong young men whom I had to dissuade from suicide when they discovered that they had contracted social disease. Others described to me their black, horrible, self-loathing, as they looked back on sordid pleasures. Yet there were many sailors who went ashore for their liberty and came back to the ship clean and strong. These men faced the same temptations. They knew the same loneliness. Their physical desires were just as strong. Yet they stood firm where others fell. The only difference I could notice was, some men were committed to a higher loyalty than taking your fun where you can find it. If your concern is to develop character, the place to begin is with your faith.

Belief In and Belief About

Once I was talking with a friend about Christianity, and he interrupted me, "I can't see that it would make the slightest difference in my actions tomorrow if I began believing everything you believe today." Though I could have suggested several desirable improvements, I did not think it the proper time to mention them, because it was, after all, a friendly discussion. As I thought about his remark, I began to discern that we were using "believe" in two senses. To me, belief in Christ meant commitment. To my friend, it meant only accepting as true some abstract theological propositions about Him. If a belief is not going to make any difference, it is hard to see why it should make any difference whether or not one believes it. When the Holy Spirit calls to you, "Believe in the Lord Jesus Christ . . ." your response ought to make a difference in your life.

Christianity is not just a set of pious thoughts about Jesus. Faith begins in the mind. But in short order it ought to infuse your emotions and your muscles. A Christian is saved, by God's grace, through his faith. His belief in the Lord Jesus Christ results in his being a member of God's family. A result like this could never flow from the kind of belief that is merely abstract and intellectual. The kind of belief that stays in the mind and never gets out to the fingertips is well expressed: "Thou believest that there is one God; thou doest well: the devils also believe, and tremble" (James 2:19). No responsible Christian would claim that thinking nice thoughts about Jesus constitutes Christian faith. A Christian believes *in* Christ.

I hold to many abstract beliefs. To mention a few: I believe that the speed of light is 186,000 miles per second. I believe that the earth is 93,000,000 miles from the sun. I believe that the star Alpha Centauri is four and one third light years distant. As far as I know, these beliefs have never made the slightest difference in the way I have done anything. This information is vitally important to the physicist. Doubtless some of it filters down to me via the mystery of electronics. But it does not in the slightest affect the way I think, talk, or act. If, tomorrow, it were announced that the speed of light is now to be officially 187,000 miles per second, I would make a note of it, but I would not work any harder, or less hard. We all hold abstract beliefs. Unhappily, many seem to think that Christian faith is one more of these pale abstractions, important only to clergymen, that filters down to the public in the form of religious holidays. Abstract belief is not in the heart, soul, and strength; it is only in the mind.

The difference between "belief about" and "belief in" lies in commitment. For example, a certain young man has definite beliefs about a young woman. He believes that she is five feet, three inches high, that she is a blonde with blue eyes, and that she is an excellent cook. These beliefs are all true, and all important. But in the course of time this young man comes to believe in her so completely that he dedicates himself to her, in the holy vows of marriage. No longer does he hold merely abstract beliefs about her. He endows her with his worldly goods. He entrusts to her his well-being and happiness for their lifetime. Fully, with no reservations, he commits himself to her, and she to him.

Another example of commitment is a person's lifework. Here are two boys, seniors in high school. Both hope to become engineers. One has a glamorous dream of himself in engineer boots and a slouch hat, puffing a short-stem pipe, grandly surveying the scene as a massive structure rises from the jungle. He has no idea how structures rise, but it looks exciting. The other boy is aware that engineering is at best 2 per cent glamor and 98 per cent mathematics. So he has taken all the work his school offers in mathematics and the sciences. He has already begun to commit himself to the gruelling preparation that must be his if ever he will be an engineer. Which of these two boys believes in engineering as a career, he who has silly romantic ideas about the work, or he who has counted the cost and has already begun to commit himself?

Christianity is the commitment of self to Christ. Of course no intelligent person would commit himself to Christ without having some true beliefs about Him. Since the Holy Spirit leads each Christian along a different path into the commitment that is Christian faith, one should be slow to generalize. So I will say only that the Philippian jailor has set a pattern for many of the adult conversions I have seen. He began by recognizing that others had something he lacked. Whatever they had gave them courage down in the pit. His Christian faith began, humanly speaking, when he reached a decision, "I want whatever it is that helps these men to sing songs in the night."

The warden turned to his Christian prisoners for information about "whatever it is that helps." They directed him, not to a philosophy of life or an organization, but to a Person. First the warden's heart was touched. Then his intellect was converted. Then he committed himself to Christ and was baptized. Significantly, his first act as a Christian, even before baptism, was a deed of kindness. He ministered to the wounds of his prisoners.

As one stands outside Christianity, examining the faith, it looks like man's wistful striving for the impossible. But when one stands within the faith, having committed himself to the service of Christ, he recognizes that this faith is no mere achievement of his own, but a gift from the Holy Spirit of God. It is given usually through the Holy Scripture, quiet meditation, and Christian contacts.

By grace are ye saved through faith; and that not of yourselves: it is the gift of God: not of works, lest any man should boast. For we are his workmanship, created in Christ Jesus unto good works, which God hath before ordained that we should walk in them.

Ephesians 2:8-10

5

THE SPIRIT IN SALVATION
Deliverance from Evil

*Brethren, ye have been called unto liberty;
only use not liberty for an occasion to the flesh,
but by love serve one another. For all the law is
fulfilled in one word, even in this; Thou
shalt love thy neighbour as thyself. But if ye bite
and devour one another, take heed that ye
be not consumed one of another. This I say then,
Walk in the Spirit, and ye shall not fulfil the
lust of the flesh. For the flesh lusteth against the
Spirit, and the Spirit against the flesh: and
these are contrary the one to the other: so
that ye cannot do the things that ye would. But
if ye be led of the Spirit, ye are not under
the law. Now the works of the flesh are
manifest, which are these; Adultery, fornication,
uncleanness, lasciviousness, idolatry, witchcraft,
hatred, variance, emulations, wrath, strife,
seditions, heresies, envyings, murders, drunkenness, revellings, and such like: of the which
I tell you before, as I have also told you in
time past, that they which do such things shall
not inherit the kingdom of God. But the fruit of*

73

the Spirit is love, joy, peace, longsuffering,
gentleness, goodness, faith, meekness, temperance:
against such there is no law. And they that are
Christ's have crucified the flesh with the
affections and lusts. If we live in the Spirit,
let us also walk in the Spirit.

GALATIANS 5:13-25

The Biblical passage above sounds, on first reading, about as contemporary as a battle communique from the War of 1812, doubtless of historical importance, but to be examined at leisure. It describes the hopeless struggle to break free from the bonds of flesh by performing works of law. Certainly this is not the language one would use to describe the contemporary struggle, where the issue is clearly marked between those who insist that man needs divine help and those who deny it. Christianity is the offer of salvation through faith in the divine Savior. The Holy Spirit's first work in salvation (logically, though not always chronologically) is to convince a person that he needs to be saved. The second step is to deliver him from the particular evils that stand between him and God.

The State of the "Flesh"

In modern English, "flesh" means muscular tissue. This kind of flesh is not bad. When the Bible says, "The flesh lusteth against the Spirit, and the Spirit against the flesh," we had better slow down and ask a few questions, before we decide what is meant.

Certainly there are grave evils in the world that rise from human physiology. The classic example is gluttony. Strange, is it not, how the modern man has come to consider gluttony as a medical problem rather than a sin? God protects the human body by the hunger mechanism. But abusing this good desire leads to evil results. Gluttony is a "sin of the flesh." There is no argument about that.

Physical desire can easily lead to grave abuse. This is the truth underlying a heresy that has dogged the church since the earliest days. When the heresy was a fully developed religion in its own right, men called it "Manichaean." For a couple centuries, the Manichaeans offered the church the stiffest opposition we faced. But, as Christians were gradually winning the victory, the Manichaeans evidently decided, "If you can't whip 'em, join 'em." At any rate, their philosophy has muddied the pure faith, off and on, ever since.

According to the Manichaeans, the material is evil, and the spiritual is good. Hence, according to the Manichaeans, even the sacred physical relationship of marriage is evil. Men have dared to call impure that which God has created, called holy, and blessed. The spiritual is not always good; for pride, jealousy, hatred, and envy are states of the spirit. And the material is not always bad. Take, for example, a slice of apple pie. In saying "The flesh lusteth against the Spirit," the Apostle Paul is not committing the Manichaean heresy. Rather he is using a technical term of early Christian theology.

"The works of the flesh are manifest. . . ." The Apostle lists fifteen sins, of which only five, by my count, rise from human physiology, and these five are all abuses of divinely implanted desire. The other ten include "idolatry, witchcraft, variance, wrath, strife, seditions, heresies, envyings." These do not rise from man's physical constitution, but rather they are tragic results of man's alienation from God. I believe no further elaboration is necessary to demonstrate that "flesh" does not mean "muscular tissue." It is a technical term of theology in the New Testament. To express the same meaning in modern English one would say, "human nature."

"The works of the flesh are manifest. . . ." Do people today behave in the appalling way that is described in the ancient world? You can quickly discover that other people act that way by turning to the newspaper. Of course not everybody is doing all of the bad things listed at once, but "wrath, strife, seditions, heresies, envyings, murders, and drunkenness" are contemporary problems. This list of human failure will prove of value to you only if you use it for the personal test. Read over the description of fallen human nature, then look into the mirror. If you do not see about six of the fifteen sins staring back at you, look harder. "What must I do to be saved?" is still a question of practical importance.

Paul gives us an operational definition of the concept "salvation." Instead of telling us what salvation *is,* he shows how an ideal saved person *acts.* "The fruit of the Spirit is love, joy, peace, longsuffering, gentleness, goodness, faith, meekness, temperance." In the fifteen ingredients of fallen human nature, one quality is conspicuously lacking, and that is love. In the nine ingredients of saved human nature, love is the cement that binds them all together. (In Christian terms love means the desire that good shall befall a person. It has little or nothing to do with infatuation and romance.) The complete love-dominated life is that of Jesus. So being saved, in the final analysis, means becoming a Christlike person.

It is scarcely necessary to say that few Christians exhibit "love, joy, peace" and the rest all the time. There is in each of us entirely too much "flesh" for that. These positive, love-filled qualities are described as the fruit of the Spirit. Fruit is the ripened product. In every Christian life the Holy Spirit has planted the seeds of love, joy, and peace. It is the Christian's task to keep the garden weeded and watered so that the fruit can grow.

Few indeed would describe the human situation today as a burning desire for release from the bonds of flesh. But on every hand one can hear cries for deliverance from the specific evils that Paul describes as "works of the flesh." So one must conclude that although the language is dated, the problem under discussion is up to date. For example, a strong man I knew succumbed to a habit that is included in Paul's list "the works of the flesh." He said to me, "I'm caught in a trap that I've made myself, and now I can't get out." That is where the human race finds itself today.

Deliverance from the "Flesh"

No one suggests that mankind should rest content with the present state of affairs: armed tension the constant order of the day; juvenile delinquency an endless, haunting problem; alcoholism a major curse; stupidity in high places; and so forth. Every observer, no matter what his faith or lack of it, can see much room for improvement in the world. Until the time of Christ, the noblest and best solution to the human dilemma was the Hebrew faith. By strict obedience to a rigid code of moral and social legislation, the devout Hebrew sought deliverance from the "flesh." As Isaiah, Amos, and Jesus all pointed out, the outward observance without the inward faith was mere hypocrisy. At its best, this program was wonderfully good; but even so, men of faith recognized that it was incomplete. The whole Old Testament breathes an intense longing for the Messiah to come and fulfill the law.

Today the chief alternative to Christian faith is called "scientific humanism." The scientific humanist seeks human welfare solely through the application of reason to man's problems. He repudiates enthusiastically all resort to the power of God. He may or may not believe in God as a metaphysical abstraction, but he considers any effort to turn to God for help or strength a sign of pitiable weakness.

For us who believe completely in the scientific approach to all problems that can be approached scientifically, the twentieth century faith poses some critical problems. One such problem is, should we consider humanism a religion? I have read bushels of arguments on the subject, and decided that the question can be argued with more heat than light. It all depends on how you define religion. As I read the works of scientific humanism, the concept holiness seems to me curiously lacking. And philosophy without holiness is not religion.

The two chief experiments in scientific humanism

during recent times have been the French Revolution and the Communist Revolution. Neither was so gratifying in its results as to urge me to seek further in that direction for salvation. But the scientific humanist explains that the next time things will be different. Science and education will cure our ills.

Wherever Christians have gone we have founded schools. Ever since the laboratory has been part of education, we have built laboratories, and fostered the search for truth through scientific methods. We believe in education. We believe in the passionate dedication to knowledge that is science. We believe that the truth will set men free from superstition, disease, ignorance, and a host of other evils. Human curiosity has searched into all imaginable corners of reality. Man has learned much, in his restless search for truth. And this is good.

Man's quest for knowledge has been so successful that the scientific humanist asks us to endorse a blank check. "Just sign here, and the method that produced penicillin will shortly produce a crime-free society." Max Otto, in his book *Science and the Moral Life* has argued brilliantly, and falsely, that science can well take over the moral prerogatives of God, and do it much more efficiently than our Creator has done. He has not, however, showed us his working model.

A recent article, "Skyhooks," in the *Harvard Business Review* examines critically some of the more outlandish pretensions of scientific humanism. The writer, Mr. O. A. Ohmann, starts with a presumption in favor of scientific education, just as I do, and concludes that man's central problem is spiritual, to be solved on his knees, not in a laboratory.

Even before the atom bomb there was a growing realization that science did not represent the whole truth, that with all its pretensions it could be dead wrong, and . . . that without proper moral safeguards the truth did not necessarily make men free. Atomic fissions intensified the fear and insecurity of every one of us who contemplated the possibility of the concentration of power in the hands of men without morals. We want science to be in the hands of men who not only recognize their responsibility to man-made ethical standards . . . but have dedicated themselves to the eternal and absolute standards of God. Thus, while the evidence of material science has been welcomed, our own personal experience will not permit us to believe that life is merely a whirl of atoms without meaning, purpose, beauty, or destiny.

The quest for knowledge is good, when directed Godward. But when it usurps the place of God, this good turns into evil. In our time the outstanding triumph of civilization has been the hydrogen bomb. That was not produced by illiterate savages, but by the best minds alive. Scientific humanism has not, to date, produced a brilliant record of spiritual achievement.

What of tomorrow? George Orwell, penetrating observer of the world, has written a novel in which he projects the present upon the immediate future. He foresees swift technological progress, at a pace so rapid that God is left behind. So man stands still, morally speaking. The novel, *1984*, is one of the most terrifying works I have ever read. It is an analysis of human nature divorced from God. George Orwell, for one, does not foresee a glorious future for "flesh."

Turn to a philosopher. Bertrand Russell is usually considered the outstanding scientific humanist of our time. He is a man of massive intellect and keen wit. It is rather surprising to find him agreeing with the Apostle Paul about anything, but on one fundamental the agreement is complete. Both say, "Humanity is doomed." Lord Russell believes that Christ cannot help. The Apostle Paul teaches that Christ makes the difference between inevitable death and eternal life. Both say, human nature has no power to save itself. Lord Russell's tragic comment:

That man is the product of causes which had no prevision of the end which they were achieving, that his origin, his growth, his hopes and his fears, his loves and his beliefs, are but the outcome of accidental collocations of atoms, that no fire, no heroism, no intensity of thought and feeling can preserve an individual life beyond the grave; but that all the labors of all the ages, all devotion, all the inspiration, all the noonday brightness of human genius, are destined to extinction in the vast death of the solar system, and that the whole temple of man's achievement must inevitably be buried beneath the debris of a universe in ruin — all these things, if not quite beyond dispute, are yet so nearly certain that no philosophy which rejects them can hope to stand. Only within the scaffolding of these truths, only on the firm foundations of unyielding despair, can the soul's habitation be safely built.

A Free Man's Worship

A Christian is obligated to examine an antagonistic viewpoint at its best, as well as its worst. Bertrand Russell is just about the best that scientific humanism can offer. He has embraced a faith with which we Christians must daily contend. In the quotation above he has scrutinized his faith, with savage honesty, and decided there is nothing ahead but the dark. He points out that all of man's beliefs, including Christianity, are but the outcome of accidental collocations of atoms. By inference, it is rather silly to believe. If that be true of my faith, is it not equally true of Lord Russell's? But that is beside the point. The point is, a keen thinker who has accepted humanism as his faith, sees only destruction ahead for humanity. So he cheers his cohorts to the fight with the battle-cry, "Despair."

The Fruit of the Spirit

The human situation is desperate. Though man can patch up some of the cracks and shore up some of the walls, man cannot save himself. The good news of the gospel is almost meaningless until one has accepted the bad news that he needs a Savior. The first step of salvation. in most cases, it the frank recognition of need. Before a man can be lifted from the mortal to the immortal plane, he must admit to himself that he needs to be lifted. When the Spirit of Christ enlightens the dark corners of a person's life, it is no longer possible for him to maintain an easygoing satisfaction with his spiritual attainments, and he turns to Christ for salvation.

The Christian belief about human nature has been called gloomy. Yet this gloomy view is confirmed over and again by the psychologist, who likewise discovers squalid depths in every man. Is it really gloomy to face the facts and then offer a solution to the problem they pose? The Holy Spirit does not leave you chained to yourself while hopelessly longing to be free.

The Holy Spirit directs one's attention both inward and outward. Within, one sees, for example, "hatred, wrath, and envy." Beyond, one sees the perfect "love, joy, and peace" that are embodied in Christ. There develops a tension between "is" and "ought to be." This tension is a normal part of Christian experience. Though I have met a few who loudly proclaim they have already achieved moral perfection, their neighbors do not confirm this report. Some tension is destructive, but other tension is creative, like the tuning of violin strings that there may be music. Here am I, chained to earth by my greed, temper, and vanity. There I ought to be, ruled completely by love, freely practicing love in every relationship of life. It is the Christian who best knows how far short he has fallen of the mark; not the skeptic who stands by and sneers at our failure, but we who strive and fail. Yet we keep on striving, in the knowledge that God has promised, "He which hath begun a good work in you will perform it" (Philippians 1:6).

The process of growth into Christian freedom has a negative and a positive aspect. Negatively, "They that are Christ's have crucified the flesh with its affections and lusts." In more prosaic terms, the Christian surrenders each sinful desire to God, somewhat as Jesus surrendered His life. If the fruit of the Spirit is to ripen within you, you must pull out the weeds. A Christian ought to submit himself to a spiritual inventory at frequent and regular intervals. In all the pages of the Bible I have found no better checklist than Galatians 5. Here are specific evils that may be found in the lives of the most respectable members of society. Almost certainly some of them are to be found in your life. Perhaps you prize them as your highest virtues. That is why each of us needs a checklist quite independent of himself. When you know what sins you are looking for, you are able to find them. Confess them. And, with the Spirit's help, root them out.

Christian conduct is more than a list of bad things not done. Christianity is positive. "The fruit of the Spirit is love, joy, peace. . . ." A successful orchardist concentrates his attention upon the growth of certain crops. The crop he hopes to produce determines his choice of pruning and cultivating methods, sprays and fertilizers. The practices that might develop beautiful peaches might well ruin an apple orchard. So the Christian ought to know what qualities of character he is supposed to grow, and concentrate on growing them.

The whole process of enlightenment, confession, aspiration, and growth is called "repentance." Mistakenly we often think that repentance means only "turning from the evil." While it definitely includes this negative aspect, it includes also "turning to the good." They that are Christ's have crucified the flesh with its affections and lusts. Beyond that, they that are Christ's have risen with Him to newness of life. And they who have entered most completely into this new life that is in Christ are first to insist that the result is not their striving after God, but the growth and development of God's Spirit within.

6

THE SPIRIT IN SALVATION

Deliverance into Life

*There was a man of the Pharisees, named
Nicodemus, a ruler of the Jews: the same came to
Jesus by night, and said unto him, Rabbi, we
know that thou art a teacher come from God:
for no man can do these miracles that thou
doest, except God be with him. Jesus answered
and said unto him, Verily, verily, I say unto
thee, Except a man be born again, he cannot see
the kingdom of God. Nicodemus saith unto
him, How can a man be born when he is old?
can he enter the second time into his mother's
womb, and be born? Jesus answered, Verily,
verily, I say unto thee, Except a man be born of
water and of the Spirit, he cannot enter into
the kingdom of God. That which is born of
the flesh is flesh; and that which is born of the
Spirit is spirit. Marvel not that I said unto
thee, Ye must be born again. The wind bloweth
where it listeth, and thou hearest the sound
thereof, but canst not tell whence it cometh and
whither it goeth: so is every one that is
born of the Spirit. Nicodemus answered and*

said unto him, How can these things be?
Jesus answered and said unto him, Art thou a
master of Israel, and knowest not these things?
Verily, verily, I say unto thee, We speak that we
do know, and testify that we have seen;
and ye receive not our witness. If I have told
you earthly things, and ye believe not, how
shall ye believe, if I tell you of heavenly things?
And no man hath ascended up to heaven, but
he that came down from heaven, even the
Son of man which is in heaven. And as Moses
lifted up the serpent in the wilderness, even
so must the Son of man be lifted up: that
whosoever believeth in him should not perish,
but have eternal life. For God so loved the
world, that he gave his only begotten Son, that
whosoever believeth in him should not
perish, but have everlasting life.

JOHN 3:1-16

If you are going to grow up you must first be born.
One would think the proposition so evident it is scarce
worth discussing, yet many have failed to grasp it. In
contrast to some twentieth century savants with whom
I have tried to discuss these matters, Nicodemus shines
as a beacon light of understanding. Of course Nicodemus had a better teacher than my friends had. The
teacher made it plain to him that there are two kinds
of life, biological and spiritual life. For either there
must be a beginning. During our days on earth, the
two interpenetrate. But finally the life that is physical
ends, and the real life that has begun on earth grows
in eternity.

The Meaning of Eternal Life

When you were born the first time, you acquired all
at once the gift of physical life, a set of parents, citizen-
ship in your country, and a host of other unearned
blessings. In all likelihood, your birth was the occasion
for rejoicing. People rejoiced in anticipation of the
good you would finally do, not that you had done anything important as yet. There can be no mature life
without birth. Describing the mystery of eternal life,
our Savior says, "You must be born again." The importance of the second birth lies not in the emotional
experience of conversion, but in the mature spiritual
life that results from being born again. Nicodemus
has asked all the obvious questions, and so made it
abundantly plain that Jesus is discussing two levels of
reality. Here He calls them "flesh" and "spirit." "Flesh"
means human nature, while "spirit" means human
nature after the touch of God's hand. Jesus sees no
present affinity between human nature (flesh) and the
divine nature (Spirit) by virtue of which man can
enter the kingdom of God. The kinship between God
and man has been smashed, beyond the possibility of
human repair. And this is the gospel message, that God
has repaired, through Christ, what man has destroyed.

In his conversation with Nicodemus, Jesus uses several interchangeable terms. He mentions "spirit," that
is, life on the level with God. He calls this life, "the
kingdom of God" and He refers to it as "eternal."
("Everlasting" in John 3:16, is a most unfortunate
translation. The same adjective is translated "eternal"
in the fifteenth verse. For reasons of literary harmony,
I suppose, the translators used the secondary meaning

when the term is repeated in the sixteenth.) "The kingdom of God" means a state of affairs in which God's will is perfectly known and completely done. They are so wrong who think of the kingdom of God, or eternal life, as something that begins when earthly life is over. You can begin to know God's will, though imperfectly, and to do His will, though imperfectly, during the course of your days on earth. He who has entered this far into the kingdom of God has entered eternal life.

Eternal does not mean endless duration. It refers to a timeless state. For example, I was talking once with a group of youngsters about the creation. A bright nine year old boy furrowed his brow and asked the inevitable question, "Who made God?" It is a sign of quick intelligence when a nine year old boy asks this question. When an adult is still asking it, you begin to wonder how hard he has tried to find the answer. I said, "Nobody made God. He is eternal. He has no beginning." The boy answered, "But everything must have a beginning." Who could quarrel with that statement? Everything must begin. But we were not discussing things; we were talking about God. So I asked, "What is two plus two?" My friend answered, "Four." This speaks well for progressive education. I asked, "And when did it become true that two plus two equals four?" This time his brow really furrowed. Finally he said, "Why, it's always been true." So here we were, confronted with a fact of cosmic importance, that had no beginning and will have no end.

In any universe the human mind can conceive, it will remain a fact that two plus two equals four. This is a timeless truth. It will be true a couple of million

years from now, and it will not be old and stale by
then. It was true before any human mind had recognized its truth, yet it is as bright and fresh today as it
ever was. This truth does not depend upon the state of
your mind, the weather, or anything else. It is quite
independent of your desires in the matter, indeed it is
independent of your very existence. This is what it
means to be eternal, to be always new and fresh, completely independent of the "ifs" that condition every
instant of earthly life. I am not equating God with the
laws of mathematics. For myself, I believe that these
laws are eternal in the sense that they are thoughts in
the mind of God, which man has begun to grasp. We
deal with eternal truth every day. It is far more profitable to think of God in eternal terms than in terms of
this world, where everything comes into being and
finally decays.

Your life had a definite beginning in time. But, by
the mystery of grace, you can be born into eternal life,
through your faith. Jesus' favorite expression for eternal
life is "the kingdom of God." The emphasis is on God's
kingship, not on man's striving. I dare say Jesus would
be rather startled to walk into one of His churches and
hear us singing:

Rise up, O men of God, the Kingdom tarries long,
Bring in the morn of brotherhood and end the
    night of wrong.

This is not Jesus' teaching. Rather, He tells us that
"The kingdom of God is at hand." You can, by faith,
become a citizen of the kingdom.

"Eternal life" means "the kingdom of God." You
need not die, physically, to enter into eternal life. May

God deliver us from a faith that works only for dead people. Christianity is a faith for the living. One who lives this earthly life to the full can know the beginnings of eternal life, to such an extent that you can say with Jesus, he is "born again."

The Need for the New Birth

"Except a man be born again, he cannot see the kingdom of God." Jesus evidently holds to the old-fashioned idea that human life is significant. What happens on earth has eternal consequences.

Whatever grows to maturity must have a beginning. Your present span of years began when you were born the first time. You were a tiny fellow, weak, so helpless that you could not even hold up your head. Doubtless you were not exactly beautiful during your first few days on earth. As you lay kicking and squalling in your cradle, you were the result of a complicated process, involving the love of a man and a woman for each other. This love, a spiritual phenomenon, had a physical expression that resulted in the complex biological process of embryonic development, as the reality that is you developed. There were months of anxiety, hours of pain — all this before you could be born. Without these, the mystery that is you could never have come into being. You must be born, of the flesh, if you are to enter human life.

Is it completely unreasonable to say that you must be born of the Spirit if you are to enter spiritual life? The cultured pagan in our time offers a vigorous dissent. He points out that his moral life, without calling on any supernatural aid, is at least as praiseworthy as that of many Christians. One could scarcely deny his contention with a straight face. It is not at all difficult to live a better moral life than the worst Christian you know. Does this affect the case at all? Your physical life was highly developed before you were born. Could not the same be said of spiritual life? Almost everyone has some good qualities. The Holy Spirit has given a measure of courage, loyalty, and honor to most people. These are spiritual qualities, and they are good wherever they may be found.

Eternal life is more than improvement of the good that is already there. When you were born the first time, your physical life had been going on for months. But the potentiality could not be realized until you were set free from the womb. There was a definite measurable moment when you quit being an embryo and became a baby. Without that release, you could never have developed into an adult.

Before a person becomes a Christian, he may well have qualities of thoughtfulness, hospitality, and kindness, for example. These wonderful qualities do not constitute him as a child of God, though they mark him as an above-average member of the human race. In order to be a child of God, there must be a definite beginning, a break with the past, an emergence into the new life. Or, as Jesus said, "You must be born again."

The cultured pagan in our time is not really contradicting Jesus on this point; he is just talking about something else. His aim is to achieve to the utmost the potentialities of man. He offers no program for entering eternal life; indeed, he denies the very possibility. He will tell you, with a deprecating smile, "Heaven and hell are right here on earth." In that statement he is correct, though his denial that they extend beyond the earth seems a little in advance of the available information. People knew just as well in Jesus' day as in ours that the earthly variety of spiritual life depends upon the proper functioning of a physical body. If a person seriously believes there is no kingdom of God into which man can enter, he is not in a position to contradict Him who says, "Except a man be born again, he cannot enter into the kingdom of God."

The second birth occurs at a definite moment in time, but we cannot always measure it with the same precision that is possible with the first birth. Some zealous Christians say there must be a sudden, sharp break with the past, that will remain forever engraved in the memory. The classic example of such a rebirth is the Apostle Paul. Yet I know many Christians who say, "I cannot recall the time when I was not a Christian." Their lives today are ample proof that they are twice born, but their memories do not recall the moment when the second birth took place. For myself, I have sufficient confidence in the Holy Spirit to leave the timing of the miracle of faith in His hands, with no advice from me. He knows, far better than I do, how best to usher each soul into the mystery of spiritual life. The fact that a person is alive is sufficient evidence that he was born.

The Source of Eternal Life

In the New Testament Greek there is a trouble-some little preposition *anothen* that has two basic meanings. Sometimes it means "again" and sometimes it means "from above." Usually the surrounding words and thoughts make completely clear which of these meanings is indicated. In Jesus' conversation with Nicodemus, either translation is possible. The translators of the Bible have rightly settled on the wording, "You must be born again." But the rest of us, who are not faced with a hard and fast choice, can well understand the phrase in its double meaning, "You must be born again from above." There is no contradiction between the two ideas. If you are to be born again, you must be born from above. The initiative in your salvation lies with God, not with you.

There are some who think this statement, that God takes the initiative in saving you, is a dismal and despairing doctrine that somehow limits human freedom. I confess I cannot join in the gloom. To me this is a source of boundless hope. You can see the bungling mess that man makes of his search for lesser goods, such as happiness. Everyone desires peace on earth, but human wisdom does not seem highly successful in achieving it. God forbid that the supreme quest of life should be left entirely up to us who have done so poorly with our other questing. Your hope for eternal life lies in God's love for you, not in your skill at finding God.

When a child is beginning to notice the world, he asks his mother one day, "Where did I come from?" If the mother is a Christian, she answers, "God sent you." It is monstrous to lie to a child with fables about the stork and other such rot. A Christian parent teaches a lesson that need not be untaught in later years. The child is not yet ready to understand the physiology of human reproduction. As he learns more and more about this subject, his increasing knowledge will but serve to illumine and glorify the answer, "God sent you."

Thou hast possessed my reins:
　　thou hast covered me in my mother's womb.
I will praise thee;
　　　for I am fearfully and wonderfully made:
　　marvellous are thy works;
　　　and that my soul knoweth right well.
My substance was not hid from thee,
　　when I was made in secret,
　　and curiously wrought in the lowest parts of the
　　　earth.
Thine eyes did see my substance, yet being un-
　　perfect;
　　and in thy book all my members were written,
　　which in continuance were fashioned,
　　　when as yet there was none of them.

Psalm 139:13-16

Is it not reasonable that God, who gave the gift of physical life, should likewise give the far more wonderful gift of spiritual life? Assuredly you did not enter this world as a result of your own planning and foresight. Likewise the way into the kingdom of God was prepared for you, long before you were ready to follow that way. You must be born from above, through the activity of the Holy Spirit, as you were first born on earth, through the activity of the Holy Spirit.

People are always trying to make the Holy Spirit conform to rules and regulations, with little visible success. It is impossible to regulate creativity; for creation means the emergence of the new. The new life that the Holy Spirit creates is a mystery. The Spirit works within the experience of each in ways that are unpredictable to man. With all the scientific psychology at our disposal, no one can tell when, or where, or how the glorious mystery of faith will operate. Jesus tells Nicodemus that the operation of the Spirit is as invisible as that of the wind. During the past few centuries we have learned much about the wind. We all know in a general way, about high pressure areas, advancing cold fronts, and that sort of thing. But the operation of the Spirit remains as mysterious as ever, when He creates in one soul after another the mystery of spiritual life.

The Way of Eternal Life

Most twentieth century readers feel a definite jar as they are reading Jesus' conversation with Nicodemus. He is talking on the highest spiritual plane, and then suddenly He mentions a snake in the desert. Frequently, the part of a Biblical discourse that sounds out of tune to us is the heart of the whole message. "As Moses lifted up the serpent in the wilderness; so must the Son of man be lifted up."

You can find the incident to which Jesus refers in Numbers 21. The children of Israel were going through the desert, grumbling, as was their custom, against their leadership, human and divine. There was a scourge of "fiery serpents." Just about every poisonous snake native to the area has been nominated for this scourge. Possibly this was the Egyptian cobra or some variety of asp or adder. Possibly the adjective "fiery" refers to the burning pain of a snake bite, possibly to the serpent's color. At any rate, there were many deaths from snake toxin. The bite of any poisonous snake is dangerous, though not always fatal. A person's attitude frequently makes the difference between death and survival. He who is crazed with fear rushes about frantically doing the wrong things, and so makes death almost certain. He who faces the disaster calmly may well pull through. Moses made a symbolic brass serpent and held it before the people. One who looked to the brazen serpent, after being bitten, was healed. This was not just glancing with the eye. It was the look of hope and confidence. The brazen serpent was an outward, visible reminder that God is triumphant over all the evils in the world. The one who held to that faith was able to fight off the poison that had been injected into his blood stream.

Compare the incident in the desert with the experience of every Christian. The serpent whose poison sickened and embittered our first parents has bitten each of us. The final result of its toxin is spiritual death. But the divine Savior has made of Himself the emblem and embodiment of evil. He has accepted the final result of man's alienation from God—suffering and death. His cross is alike the symbol and the reality of evil. He died there that you might be born from above. And what is your part in the new birth? Your part is the look of faith, to believe in the Lord Jesus Christ. This is not just belief in the sense of abstract thought about Him, but belief with the heart and the strength, as well as the mind. Your part in the new birth is looking to Christ in confidence that He can create a new life within you. You can stifle the growth and development of that new life, if you will. Or, you can grow into what your heavenly Father designed for you to become, a spirit who will live eternally.

So endeth Jesus' conversation with Nicodemus. Then the Evangelist John summarized the conversation in what is probably the most powerful sentence ever written: "God so loved the world, that he gave his only begotten Son, that whosoever believeth in him should not perish, but have eternal life."

7

THE SPIRIT IN SALVATION
The Baptism of the Spirit

*And when the day of Pentecost was fully come,
they were all with one accord in one place.
And suddenly there came a sound from heaven as
of a rushing mighty wind, and it filled all
the house where they were sitting. And there
appeared unto them cloven tongues like as of
fire, and it sat upon each of them. And they were
all filled with the Holy Ghost, and began to
speak with other tongues, as the Spirit gave
them utterance. And there were dwelling at
Jerusalem Jews, devout men, out of every
nation under heaven. Now when this was noised
abroad, the multitude came together, and were
confounded, because that every man heard
them speak in his own language. And they
were all amazed and marvelled, saying one to
another, Behold, are not all these which speak
Galileans? And how hear we every man in our
own tongue, wherein we were born? Parthians,
and Medes, and Elamites, and the dwellers in
Mesopotamia, and in Judaea, and Cappadocia, in
Pontus, and Asia, Phrygia, and Pamphylia, in*

Egypt, and in the parts of Libya about Cyrene,
and strangers of Rome, Jews and proselytes,
Cretes and Arabians, we do hear them speak in
our tongues the wonderful works of God.
And they were all amazed, and were in doubt,
saying one to another, What meaneth this?
Others mocking said, These men are full of
new wine. But Peter, standing up with the eleven,
lifted up his voice, and said unto them. . . .
ACTS 2:1-14

We have looked briefly at three steps in a Christian's
spiritual development: first, the awareness of need;
second, the emergence from "flesh"; third, the emergence into "spirit." There follows a fourth step, "the
baptism of the Spirit." These steps do not always
proceed in this neat, logical order; since God who
made us all different insists upon treating us as indi-
viduals. We may roughly describe the baptism of the
Spirit as a heightened awareness of God's presence
within a person's life. I find in the Holy Scripture
no precise verbal definition for the baptism of the
Spirit, but I find many operational definitions, none
more glorious than that recorded in the second chapter
of Acts.

A Case Study in the Baptism of the Spirit

Our Savior's disciples were gathered in an upper
room in Jerusalem. We may suppose, with some confidence, that these were the five hundred whom the
Apostle Paul mentions in I Corinthians 15:6. They
were met because they loved the Lord Jesus Christ.
Then, "Suddenly there came a sound from heaven as
of a rushing mighty wind, and it filled all the house

where they were sitting. And there appeared unto them cloven tongues like as of fire, and it sat upon each of them." Just what did that fire look like? The few artists daring enough to paint this scene have produced results that are far from solemn and awe-inspiring. For they try to picture the fire as the sort of stuff with which we are completely familiar, in which carbon and oxygen unite to form carbon dioxide plus smoke plus heat. What is this kind of fire? When the flames descended, were the curtains in danger? Or was this the flame of God's love?

I have never known anyone who "saw" the fire of God. But I have known hundreds and read of thousands whose baptism of the Spirit can be described only in terms of flame. Take as an example the experience of Blaise Pascal. Though he never quite left the communion of the Roman Catholic Church, Pascal was a formative thinker of Protestant theology. He was a seminal mathematician, and one of the chief architects of modern philosophy. As if that were not glory enough for any man, he was an outstanding mechanical engineer. He discovered the principle of barometric pressure, invented the hydraulic press and the adding machine. Yet to him, these honors were trivial in contrast to his knowledge that the Spirit had baptized him. Sewed in the lining of his cloak, Pascal carried a parchment, inscribed in his own precise hand, where he recorded as it were a stenographic report of baptism by the Holy Spirit:

In the year of grace 1654, on Monday 23rd of November . . . from about half past ten in the evening until about half past twelve

FIRE

God of Abraham, God of Isaac, God of Jacob,
   not of the philosophers and scholars.
Certitude. Certitude. Feeling. Joy. Peace.
God of Jesus Christ . . .
I have separated myself from Him. I have fled
   from Him, denied Him, crucified Him.
Let me never be separated from Him. We keep
   hold of Him only by the ways taught in the
   Gospel.
Renunciation, total and joyous
Total submission to Jesus Christ. . . .

Every Protestant knows the story of John Wesley,
who wrote of the corresponding episode in his own
life, "I felt my heart strangely warmed within me." It
is almost impossible to. describe the baptism of the
Spirit without mentioning fire, warmth, or light.

Fire and Emotion

God's flaming love burned within our fathers, and
it seemed that their faces were ablaze. They were
excited. They had something to be excited about. As
they poured out into the street, some derisively hooted,
"These men are full of new wine." Religious emotion
is part of Christian faith. Protestants have gone to
extremes in both directions. Some have said, in
effect, that emotion is the all-important part of faith.
Others, recoiling against excess in the name of Christ,
have apparently decided to remove emotion from
faith altogether.

From the Apostle Paul's letters to the Corinthians,
it is quite apparent that there were crude excesses of

emotionalism in the early church, and the Apostle was deeply disturbed by them. On the first day of Pentecost, the members of the church began speaking in tongues. Since a foreign tongue sounds like meaningless babble to one who does not understand, members of the Corinthian church would sometimes babble incoherently, and explain "I am speaking in tongues." So here the Apostle faces a dilemma. To condemn speaking in tongues would be to deny the power of God. But to encourage the practice would mean the end of rational Christianity. His practical conclusion is: "I had rather speak five words with my understanding . . . than ten thousand words in an unknown tongue" (I Corinthians 14:19).

There are Christians in the world today whose faith is an orgy of religious emotionalism. Sometimes they call the emotions the "baptism of the Holy Spirit." In the New Testament, you find much about the baptism of the Holy Spirit. You find that this baptism is always accompanied by deep emotion — under control. But you never find anyone urging that others seek religious excitement for its own sake. If it is excitement you are after, let me recommend a ride on the roller coaster. It only costs a quarter. The baptism of the Holy Spirit costs a life. The life will be filled with emotion, but the emotion will be productive of results.

Fire — and here I mean the friction of molecules — is one of God's outstanding gifts to man. But it is a dangerous blessing. Unless channeled and directed, fire is destructive. And so the flame of God's Spirit must be channeled and directed, both inward and outward. Inwardly, the one enlightened grows in knowledge and love of God. But Christianity can never stop there.

Our faith must spread into the community round about. When an engineer has built up a fire in the boiler, and generated a head of steam, he has only begun his work. He generates the steam because work must be done in the world. So the emotion that accompanies illumination by the Holy Spirit serves two basic purposes: First, it enables one to care for others, and second, it enables one to break through the barriers that divide him from his neighbor.

Breaking Through the Language Barrier

As our fathers met together there were devout people from all over the Mediterranean world who had gathered in Jerusalem for the high holy day. The majority of the strangers in town had come to worship God.. Some had come to make an honest dollar. Some were there to pick pockets. The Holy Spirit stirred our fathers to care for these people, so that they would risk ridicule and physical danger to convey the good news about Jesus Christ. The baptism of the Holy Spirit means, in large part, "concern." Concern had its dangers. After all, Jesus was crucified in Jerusalem, just a few weeks before. The same evil men who crucified Him were still walking about, still dangerous. Beyond this was a practical barrier to communication. Our fathers were Galileans. The strangers were Parthians, Medes, Elamites, Mesopotamians, Cappadocians, Egyptians, Greeks, Arabians, and Romans. Between the Christians and the neighbor, for whom Christ died, was a barrier of language.

Although you can express much by smiles and gestures, there is much more that can be expressed only by words. Put this sentence into smiles and gestures, if you can: "God so loved the world that he gave his only begotten Son, that whosoever believeth in him should not perish but have everlasting life." This sentence is the message that our fathers must convey to the foreigners. The problem of communication is nothing new. The language barrier is as old as the diversity of human speech.

I do not know how the Holy Spirit enabled our fathers to break through the language barrier. But I can tell you how, in the recent past, the Spirit worked in the life of a modern Christian to achieve much the same result. This twentieth century saint was sent as a missionary to Arabia. Before beginning his work he took a full year to study the language. He used an Arabic-English dictionary and a grammar, under the guidance of a language instructor. At the end of the year, he still spoke Arabic with a strong Nebraska accent, but he could make his way around. More important, he could proclaim the unsearchable mystery of Christ, in words that his hearers could understand. His devoted toil and study were the work of the Holy Spirit who empowered our fathers to speak with the Parthians, Medes, and Elamites. We shall not know, until we meet them in heaven, exactly how our fathers were helped to break through the invisible curtain. That is no practical concern of ours. There are, however, two points that we should remember: (1) a barrier was there, and (2) they broke through. The Bible describes this break-through as the work of the Holy Spirit.

The Spirit and the Translations

As you look at the record, it is impossible to repress

a thrill of joy at the work the Holy Spirit has been
doing, for nineteen long centuries, to enable your
fathers and brothers in Christ to continue breaking
through the language barrier.

Early in the second century the church faced a
practical problem, how to carry the gospel to the north.
At that time most of the church members were Greek-
speaking. The New Testament was written in Greek.
But the neighbors to the north spoke Syriac. It was not
difficult to see what needed to be done, though it must
have been quite difficult to do it. Apparently a scholar
named Tatian was the first to undertake the task. He
compiled a Syriac life of Christ from our four Gospels.
Not long after, some unknown scholars translated the
entire New Testament into the Syriac tongue. This
was the Bible for the Nestorian Christians, who spread
the gospel from Persia into Arabia, India, Turkestan,
and China. Christianity did not survive in China,
possibly because the missionaries did not translate the
Scripture into Chinese.

The God-given work, translating the Holy Scripture,
was carried on brilliantly during the earliest Christian
centuries. It culminated in the magnificent Latin translation made by Jerome. It is one of the major tragedies
of Christian history that this translation, designed to
give people the Scripture in their own tongue, gradually
became a barrier to the people, something to be read
only by the clergy. The work of translation, so brilliantly begun, ground almost to a halt, until the
Protestant Reformation set man free, once more, to
search the Scripture. This freedom carries with it the
sacred obligation to translate.

By now, the entire Bible has been translated into 191 different languages. The entire New Testament is in 246. Parts of the Bible have been translated into 1,109 tongues, and in 650 of them publication is going on today. The difference between 1,109 and 650 can be explained in two words, "dead languages." For example, the first Bible published in the Western Hemisphere was in the Massachusetts language. Today nobody speaks that tongue. It would be futile to publish in it.

Every once in a while, some good-hearted soul writes to the American Bible Society suggesting:

I would be so glad to help in the translating of the Bible, and so if you would send me a dictionary and a grammar of some of these primitive languages, I would be happy to dedicate my spare time to the translation of the New Testament.

Eugene Nida,
God's Word in Man's Language,
Harper and Brothers,
p. 56

It is not quite so simple. It took Jerome thirty-four years to translate the Old Testament into Latin, and that was his native tongue. To translate into a foreign tongue often takes much longer. There are no dictionaries and grammars for many primitive languages. If you would translate the New Testament into some obscure Guatemalan dialect, for instance, you need the baptism of the Holy Spirit. The Spirit will fill you with concern for others, concern so deep and intense that you must leave your home and go to live for years in the jungle. You will learn quite rapidly that primitive languages are not simple. English, German, Chinese, Greek: these are the simple languages. Their complexities have been broken down by centuries of civilization. Our uncivilized dialect is really complicated. Doubtless you will have to invent an alphabet. Then you will need to reduce the complexities of the language to a system. The system is there. It is up to you to discover it. Then you will need to learn the idiom, those thousands of exceptions to the rule you have so carefully exposed. By this time you will know the language so well you can see that your first ten years' labor are inferior, and must be done again. After a lifetime, you will be able to turn your notebooks over to your successor, and he can make the translation.

Why should anyone go to all that bother for a lot of unimportant savages? For the professional linguist the question is answered. But the Bible is seldom translated by professional linguists. It is translated by Christians who have received the baptism of the Holy Spirit. They care enough to master an alien science because of their concern for others. In the vocabulary of the Holy Spirit, there are no unimportant people in the world. Some live on a high plane of material culture, others on a primitive plane. But they are all people. And each needs the inspired Word of God.

The easy translations were made centuries ago. Only difficulties remain. Yet there are more devout servants of God working at the task of Bible translation today than ever before in history. The Holy Spirit has taught them to care for those on the other side of the invisible curtain, and caring, to convey the gospel.

Buttonhole Evangelism

Our class in seminary was studying the record of the first Pentecost. A good friend of mine jotted in the margin of his notebook, "Peter preached one sermon, and won three thousand converts. What's the matter with our preaching today?" That's a preacher for you! Peter's sermon was good, but not that good. Our fathers, out in the street, had done some powerful and effective personal evangelism before Peter began to speak. If we are right in placing their number at five hundred, then on the average, each won six converts to Christ. Six is a number I can understand. Three thousand is just a big, vague blur.

As you study the records of "mass evangelism" in our time, you find that those who have been most successful in reaching the masses have been preceded and followed by those who minister, less conspicuously, to the individual. Communication to the "masses," whether by Peter, speaking to several thousand, or Dr. Graham, speaking to several million, is important; but it can never take the place of the individual Christian speaking with his neighbor.

To master our obscure Guatemalan dialect requires first that you care enough to do the work, then that you do the work. This takes an investment of years. Strangely enough, you have invested years in the mastery of a difficult language. You know its subtle twists of inflection, its massive and expressive vocabulary. I am referring to the English language. And by an odd coincidence, there is living near you a neighbor, who speaks the same language you do to whom the name of

Christ is but a curse. It is a Christian's elementary duty to communicate to this neighbor the message of God's love in Christ. If you have not done your part to carry this message, you might say that a barrier exists, though it is not one of language.

The barrier I find most often is one the Christian erects within himself. You might call it the "shyness barrier." As a good Christian put it, "I just don't want to be a religious fanatic." God knows, I do not want you to be one either. You who are laymen try to be somewhere else when the religious fanatic shows up. Try to imagine how we clergymen feel about them; for we see five to your one. They turn off their minds and turn on their tongues, transfix us with their beady eyes, call us liars, hypocrites, and scoundrels, and then wonder plaintively why we do not rush off to get saved their way. Christianity has grown in the world in spite of religious fanatics. We certainly do not need any more. The church needs people of calm, reasonable judgment, who have a sense of humor, who can keep quiet while the other person is talking, but still can progress toward a goal. We need people who are filled with the Holy Spirit; so full that His love overflows their lives and turns them toward the neighbor. We need people who have a radiant faith, and that means, by definition, a faith that radiates — to your neighbor — from you.

"But I Don't Feel That Way"

Many Christians understand perfectly when the Bible speaks of the fire of God entering the lives of men. Others, equally sincere, say to me, "That's all very well, but I never felt that way." Neither had the members of the early church until the first day of Pentecost, neither had Pascal until the 23rd of November, neither had John Wesley until the Aldersgate experience. Yet each of these saints was in the communion of the church, each was consciously trying to do God's will when the Holy Spirit flamed within his soul. Sometimes, though not often, the Spirit inflames the heart of one who is actively defying God's will, as happened in the case of the Apostle Paul. And there are millions of Christians, of whom I know many hundreds, whose lives are aflame with God's love, and yet they never experienced any definite moment of illumination.

We Presbyterians have a saying, "The Holy Spirit moveth where, and when, and how He chooseth." There is no set pattern a Christian's religious experience must follow. To you who are troubled by doubts and uncertainties, I pass on the words that meant so much to Pascal, during a similar time in his life, "Thou wouldst not be seeking me, if I had not found thee." The fact that you are seeking is a sign that the flame of God's love already burns within you.

Still, there are many who long for the overpowering assurance of God's presence in their lives, with such a manifestation as the apostles in the early church knew. Can they develop their awareness of God? The story is told about William Turner, the British painter whose sunsets are riotous blazes of color. A friend remarked to him, "I never see colors like that in the sky." And Mr. Turner answered, correctly but cruelly, "Don't you wish you could?" He need not have stopped there. Any person with normal vision can learn to see all the colors of the spectrum, and he can discover for himself that God's painting in the western sky makes Turner's painting on canvas look drab and pale. It takes time and concentration, but a person who is not color-blind can develop his color sense.

So it is possible for each of us to develop his consciousness of God. This comes, not through any magic formula or mystic rites, but through simple obedience to the known will of Christ. After all, Jesus never said, "Feel thus and so." Often He has told us, "This do." To the one who does His will, year in and year out, the Savior has made a promise, "If ye then, being evil, know how to give good gifts unto your children: how much more shall your heavenly Father give the Holy Spirit to them that ask him?" (Luke 11:13).

8

THE DIFFERENCE FAITH MAKES

In Time of Disaster

> *Now when they had gone throughout Phrygia and the region of Galatia, and were forbidden of the Holy Ghost to preach the word in Asia, after they were come to Mysia, they assayed to go into Bithynia: but the Spirit suffered them not. And they passing by Mysia came down to Troas. And a vision appeared to Paul in the night; There stood a man of Macedonia, and prayed him, saying, Come over into Macedonia, and help us. And after he had seen the vision, immediately we endeavored to go into Macedonia, assuredly gathering that the Lord had called us for to preach the gospel unto them.*

ACTS 16:6-10

Paul and Silas hoped, above all else, to proclaim the gospel in the province of Asia (what we call Asia Minor). And the Holy Spirit prevented their doing so. Once in a Sunday School class I said this and a young skeptic snorted, "The Holy Spirit! I'd bet it was a policeman." To his considerable surprise, I agreed with him. As far as the outward eye could see, there was no visible constraint from the Holy Spirit. Some have suggested disease, some have suggested travel difficulties, my own guess is that a military policeman blocked the way into Bithynia. It does not matter, as far as we are concerned, what natural agent stood between the Christians and their goal. The question before us is rather, "What difference does Christian faith make when the world turns upside down?"

The Christian seeks and finds God's light, whatever the darkness that may engulf him. Paul and Silas are deeply disappointed, of course. How do they accept disappointment? Do they sit around and sulk? Do they vent their feelings in hatred for the policeman? Do they turn to other honorable pursuits, concluding they have given God His chance? No. They decide, "The Holy Spirit prevented us." They accept a disappointment as God's way of leading them to a right decision.

Paul and Silas were stopping in Troas, thwarted in their desire to carry the gospel to Bithynia. Then Paul had a vision. A man from across the Aegean Sea appeared to him, saying, "Come over into Macedonia and help us." And they who had hoped to preach the gospel in another Asian city went instead to the European continent. Though the Christian church was born in what we call Asia, the stormy adolescence of our faith was in Europe, and on that continent the church grew to maturity. Only in quite recent centuries has the church returned in force to the continent of her birth. Speaking from the human vantage point, Paul and Silas are responsible for bringing the gospel to Europe. They brought the message there because God refused them permission to carry the gospel to Bithynia.

They recognized that "No" is never the final answer
for God. God closed one door of opportunity to them
because He willed to open another, and better, door.

Disappointment As a Fact of Life

Christians ought to face disappointment creatively.
We believe that finally God will triumph over all evil.
But our faith did not rise in vacuum; it rose and grew
in a world where often it appears that evil has tri-
umphed over God. Theologians have subdivided evil
into two major classes, the "natural" and the "moral."
A natural evil is one for which no man bears any
known responsibility, such as an earthquake or a hurricane. A moral evil is one for which man is entirely
responsible, such as the sin of snobbery. Most evils of
our acquaintance are a mixture of both natural and
moral evil. There is much tragic man-caused sickness
or injury brought on by pollution of the water and
air, by carelessness in handling food, by cheapening
the mystery of procreation, by the destructive consump-
tion of alcohol, and by the thoughtless use of heavy
machinery. The outstanding evils in our time are
war and hunger. Both are compounded of natural
evil and moral wrong. Most evil brings in its wake
keen disappointment to someone. We are considering
the question: How does a Christian face such disappointment? What difference does our faith make
when life caves in?

The fashionable alternatives to our Christian way
of looking at disaster are rather depressing. Through
some fast verbal juggling, one is supposed to be persuaded that things are not quite so bad as they seem.
When the juggling is over, though, they still look the

same to most of us. The alternatives you are likely to hear today are:

Take the Long-Range View. Sometimes it is shortness of vision that leads us to proclaim something as evil. For example, a panther kills a deer and eats it. From the deer's viewpoint that is remarkably bad. In the Kaibab Forest, on the north rim of the Grand Canyon, some misguided conservationists decided to befriend the deer. Just why deer are more deserving of human friendship than panthers was never made clear to me. The conservationists, with the best intentions in the world, killed off the panthers. Freed from their natural enemy, the deer multiplied and multiplied. After a short time, they had eaten all the low browse, then they ate the high browse. Then they nibbled away the moss, and then the bark. After that, there was nothing left to eat; so they starved. The beautiful animals that had been saved from the panthers became food for the buzzards. The moral of the story is: A panther is a deer's best friend.

Some moralists have decided that all evil is comparable. Just take the long-range viewpoint, and what looks bad will appear to be good. I gather that time is supposed to be the catalyst that makes the difference. Unfortunately, most of us cannot wait three or four centuries to see our problems in perspective. We have to work on the solutions now. How long must my viewpoint get for me to discover the good in addiction to narcotics?

Illusion. Others have decided that all evil is illusion. Unquestionably, much evil has been just that. Intelligent people used to be tortured by fear of the dead.

When they heard ghastly noises in the attic, they genuinely thought that ghosts were making them. Today we send for a plumber to locate the gurgle in the drainpipe. Once you recognize something as harmless, it can no longer harm you *if* you are correct in your judgment. Admit that the noise in the attic is caused by the plumbing, and it is merely annoying, no longer terrifying. You have opened your mind, and the evil has flown. Unhappily, the same solution does not seem to work quite so well with such evils as war, political slavery, and alcoholism. Take a long, thoughtful walk through the ward at your State hospital, where men created in the image of God are living out a vegetable existence, their humanity destroyed by syphilis. If you can still contend that evil is an illusion, I congratulate you for having a remarkable illusory apparatus.

Relativity. The theory of relativity deals with the speed of light and related phenomena. Unfortunately, each major scientific theory seems to attract bustling philosophers who try to make it apply to everything, whether it applies or not. So the moral relativist points out that it all depends on your viewpoint. Of course he can make a case. Consider, for example, a minor tragedy. A fox slips into the chicken coop and eats a hen. The farmer is quite definitely annoyed. From the fox's viewpoint, though, the episode was a remarkable success. Before we give way to rejoicing with the fox, let us consider the hen's attitude. Each of these viewpoints is completely valid. It's all relativity.

Most of us will continue to survey the human situation through human eyes. It would be true, but tactless, to show that the tragic death of a loved person represents a remarkable triumph for a particular variety of microbe.

A friend of mine who calls himself a moral relativist seems to forget about his theory when he confronts a ghastly evil like Buchenwald. He forgets that this shameful butchery of human life looked good, from the viewpoint of the Nazis. My friend tells me learnedly that "wrong" is just a word to describe what I do not like, yet he joins me in condemning the "wrongs" of tyranny. He thinks on a higher plane than he talks.

There is a basic difference between good and bad, right and wrong. However we may differ about the details, some knowledge of good and evil remains in each of us. In a time like ours, we cannot stomach a Pollyanna faith that ignores or belittles the gravity of evil in the world. Neither dare we give way to a pessimism that concedes victory to the devil. We need a faith that will enable us to meet the disappointments and disasters of life manfully. And that is exactly what our faith in the crucified Savior offers. Jesus died on a cross, to help people like us in our battles against evil. He gasped in real pain, He wept salt tears, He knew real heartbreak. Those who loved Him received the most bitter disappointment in history. But God led them out of the darkness into the light.

The Christian church holds that good finally will triumph over the evil. This is the message so vividly portrayed in the closing book of the Bible, the Revelation. Here we see strife, anguish, and confusion, but out of it all, Christ arises triumphant. This is the faith to which the Christian clings while he faces the disappointments and sorrows of daily life. They are evils, genuine and real, but they are not, and cannot be the final word. The last word, for Christians, is Christ, Victor over every power of darkness.

Without God, disappointment is final. A friend of mine was a hospital porter, a man of limited education, but of uncompromising honesty. One day he helped carry a little girl to what proved to be her deathbed. He stood and looked at her for a while, then announced to the nurse, "No God worth his salt would let things like this happen." With that he quit his position in the hospital. His attitude is honest, one can say that much for it. It faces the fact of evil squarely and frankly. And its final outcome can be nothing but despair. "Things like this" keep happening. Once you eliminate God from the picture, then evil must necessarily have the last word. Man will build his cities, and they will be destroyed. Man will compose his songs, but in time no one will sing them. Each man will die. Finally all earthly life will die. Then there will be no more pain to be sure. But likewise there will be no laughter, love, or loyalty. Death will be triumphant over life. Evil will have the last word. Without God, there is no hope for the long view, just

> take the cash and let the credit go
> nor heed the rumble of the distant drum.

When You Walk Through the Storm

Paul and Silas faced a bitter disappointment. They wanted to do God's holy will. They believed it God's will for them to preach the gospel in Bithynia. They made every possible effort to get there. And each effort was blocked. Instead of giving way to their discourage-

ment, they continued to seek for opportunities to do
God's will, and found them. A short time later, when
other missionaries preached the gospel in Bithynia, the
church of Christ was established and growing on the
European continent. God had "led" his servants to
Europe, by blocking them from Bithynia.

Sometimes we sing about the Spirit's guidance
through life:
I ask no dream, no prophet ecstasies,
    No sudden rending of the veil of clay,
No angel visitant, no opening skies,
    But take the dimness of my soul away.

Paul and Silas had sufficient clarity of spiritual vision
to recognize that their bitter disappointment did not
mean God was defeated. No angel descended to inform
them that God had other, and better, plans for them.
Their faith had taught them to see the Holy Spirit's
activity, even in their disappointment. So, when the
dream came, they were ready to act.

The disappointments of life come on all levels of
seriousness. When it comes to trifles, a Christian ought
to shrug them away as trifles. "Oh dear, it's raining
and I can't go to the ball game." Well, that's too bad.
Stay at home and read a good book. There follow
several stories, all true, of people who have met disaster
and learned that Christ comes in the clouds. I have
known those who have faced similar disappointments,
and become miserable, cynical, and embittered. Paul
and Silas had a disappointment that was measured in
weeks. These that follow are measured in lifetimes.

A career destroyed. In 1839 a young naval officer,
Lieutenant Matthew Maury, was travelling to a new

assignment aboard the brig *Consort,* to survey the southern harbors of the eastern seaboard. Lieutenant Maury was recognized throughout the navy as a young man to watch, on the way up. Then the stagecoach upset. Lieutenant Maury suffered a dislocation of the right knee, a fracture of the thigh bone. In a few seconds of tragedy, a career at sea became impossible. He was a cripple.

The Secretary of the Navy granted Mr. Maury an honorable sinecure as Superintendent of the Depot of Charts and Instruments. At the age of thirty-six, Matthew Maury was on the shelf. What difference does faith make? Matthew Maury was a devout Christian. He said that in boyhood he learned "to love the truth and always to remember God." There on the shelf he had ample opportunity to do both. He might so easily have become bitter and cynical, but instead he sought for the truth where he was, and not where he wished he might have been. The Spirit led him to study the dust-covered logs of ships that had travelled the seas he no longer could sail. And gradually a conclusion crystallized in his mind:

> There are rivers in the sea. They are of such magnitude that the mightiest streams of the land are rivulets compared to them. They are either of warm or cold water, while their banks and beds are water of the opposite temperature. For thousands of miles they move through their liquid channels unmixed with the confining waters. They are the horizontal movements called currents.

This is old stuff to us; we learned it in grade school. It was news to the experienced sea captains a century ago.

In 1853 Mr. Maury's theory was put to a dramatic proof. Off the New Jersey coast the *San Francisco,* heavily laden with passengers, was struck by a hurricane, dismasted, and left a derelict. Matthew Maury studied the winds and currents of the area, pencilled a blue cross on his chart and said to the Secretary of the Navy, "Here she will likely be found." And the rescue ships located the derelict at the precise spot that Mr. Maury had indicated.

Matthew Maury chose a career of service at sea, and that door of opportunity was closed to him. Instead of giving up in despair, he looked for other opportunities to serve, and he found them. Of all the men who entered the naval service in 1825, it is safe to say that Matthew Maury made the largest contribution to his country. Where he could not sail the sea, he studied it, and ever since navigators have thanked him. Through his studies the average length of a trip around the Horn from New York to San Francisco was reduced by fifty days. This is not just a story of human spirit triumphant. It is a story of the Spirit of God, working through the human spirit, opening a door of scientific inquiry by first closing a door of active service at sea.

On the banks of the Maury River, the State of Virginia has erected a memorial shaft where the inscription reads, in part:

EVERY MARINER FOR COUNTLESS AGES
AS HE TAKES HIS CHART
TO SHAPE HIS COURSE ACROSS THE SEAS
WILL THINK OF THEE
HIS INSPIRATION HOLY WRIT

The inspiration God brought to Matthew Maury through the Holy Scripture is still available to you who would face disappointment creatively today.

A Life Taken. A wonderful friend has given me permission to quote the following letter, written some months after the events described:

Your letters have meant much to me during the past few lonely months, and more letters are still coming in from friends all over the world who knew and loved my sweet Bet. It is not easy for me to write even yet, but I must thank you, and let you know something of the joy and faith the two of us shared through the pain, and after when all that had made my life happy and warm and beautiful was gone.

It was in October following a wonderful, happy summer, that we were first shocked by the discovery of the recurrence of cancer — such a sudden massive recurrence that after one quick look our friend and doctor came from the examining room and told me there was no hope. He took it hard. Everyone who knew Bet loved her. He could not even bear to go back and tell her the news, but asked me to do so. Of the rest of that day, I remember very little, except that Bet was not afraid. Then came three weeks of X-ray treatments and the sudden relapse that sent her to the hospital in an ambulance. That was the second week in November.

As I look at the weeks in the hospital I remember best the times we read the Bible together.

Every day, clear up to the end, Bet would repeat in her soft southern way the 103rd Psalm:

> Bless the Lord, O my soul, and all that is within me bless His Holy Name. Bless the Lord, O my soul, and forget not all His benefits — who forgiveth all thine iniquities; *who healeth all thy diseases.* . . .

Those confident words we took as God's Word to us. We began to read together every record we could find in the Gospels of how Jesus healed the sick. I had forgotten how full of miracles of healing the Gospels are. As we read, our hope returned and we began to pray together definitely and earnestly, knowing that the Lord who loved her could heal her.

But He didn't heal her. The second week in January the surgeon operated to relieve some of the pain, and four days later, on January 17, at three in the morning, she left me. Her last word was whispered "Amen," joining mine as I prayed with her just before she slipped into the coma from which she did not return.

That night, when it was all over and I stumbled back to M——'s, I had another unexpected word from her. The day before the operation she had said to Isabel M——, "Tell Sam, if the operation does not go as we are hoping, to remember that what God does is perfect." Then she paused, and added, "And tell him that the last twelve years have been the happiest years of my life." I will never cease to marvel that there in the midst of her own suffering Bet somehow managed to think ahead unselfishly to what I would need most just then — the memory of the sheer joy that being together had always meant to us, and the reminder that when we cannot understand, we can still trust. "What God does is perfect." It would have been easy to lose faith then, but for that reminder. We had been so confident that she would be healed. We had prayed in faith. But the prayer of faith that heals is a gift of God; we do not manufacture it by our earnestness. There would be something pitiful about our confidence there in the hospital but for the fact that it too was a gift of God. It brought us through the long dark suffering days not with a spirit of despair, but with a feeling of expectancy and confidence. Clear up to the end we knew that the Lord could heal her, and that knowledge buoyed us up with hope, and we trusted Him. When He did not heal her, and the darkness came in close and cold, the trust remained. For His way is perfect, and we know there is a greater miracle even than the miracle of healing. There is the Resurrection. . . .

Sam

You can readily understand Sam's reluctance to permit me to publish so intensely personal a letter as this. Even so, he graciously gave his permission, because many families are called to go through similar darkness, and not all of them have a faith that will give light. Man's central need, always and everywhere, is a living bond with his Creator. In the anguish of bitter sorrow, one becomes intensely aware of this need. I am grateful to Sam for sharing his letter with you, because you need a faith like his. The letter is not theorizing about the value of faith, it is a vivid testimonial to the power and glory of that faith, when all else has failed.

A defective child. Probably you are familiar with the story of Roy and Dale Evans Rogers, and their little daughter, Robin Elizabeth. When Robin was born, the doctors recognized her as a borderline Mongoloid, a baby who could never, humanly speaking, develop into a normal woman. We who minister to the bereaved often are asked, "Why do things like this happen?" Often we have seen comparable sorrows turn people into bitterness. In her touching account of Robin's life, Mrs. Rogers makes it clear that the little child was not the one who suffered, but those who loved her. And in the valley of the shadow she discovered also that suffering has a redemptive purpose. In the foreword to her book, *Angel Unawares* (Fleming H. Revell Co.), Mrs. Rogers says:

> I believe with all my heart that God sent her on a two-year mission to our household, to strengthen us spiritually and to draw us closer together in the knowledge and love and fellowship of God. It has been said that tragedy and sorrow never leave us where they find us. In this instance, both Roy and I are grateful to God for the privilege of learning some great lessons of truth through His tiny messenger, Robin Elizabeth Rogers.

Here is the New Testament faith about disappointment. Mr. and Mrs. Rogers, like every other honorable family, longed and prayed that their daughter might grow into normal womanhood. But when God said "No" to that prayer, they accepted His answer with

gratitude. If ever you have seen a Mongoloid child,
Mrs. Rogers' word "grateful" surely hit you with a
shock. When tragedy strikes, the best advice the world
can offer is "Resignation." Gratitude is for Christians.
Resignation leads to apathy. Christian gratitude leads
to sympathy with others who are facing the same
problem. Mrs. Rogers, for example, has devoted the
considerable royalties from her book to the National
Association for Retarded Children, to help others face
one of life's major disasters constructively.

Faith Betrayed. You will notice that these tragedies are
listed in what I believe to be the descending order.
The ultimate, I believe, is betrayal by one who is
loved. To most people today, not only to Christians,
Judas Iscariot is a far more loathsome specimen than
Attila the Hun. Attila slew his thousands, and Judas
was responsible for the death of only One. But Attila
killed his enemies, while Judas betrayed his Friend.

The story is familiar enough. A boy, born into a
good family, given every advantage of culture and
education, turned sour. His acts of boyish mischief
grew less and less mischievous, more and more vicious.
Warnings and admonitions failed, and finally the boy
was imprisoned. The father died, quite literally, of a
broken heart. The mother, a woman of quiet and
courageous Christian faith, kept on praying. For years
on end the prayers appeared to be unanswered. The
young man would serve his two to five years and be
released. He would promise to go straight, and keep
the promise faithfully for at least six months. Then
another arrest. Apparently he had no conscience at all,
in regard to matters like truthfulness or financial in-

tegrity. He seemed to take a positive delight in betraying those who tried hardest to help him. And still the mother prayed that God would redeem her son. By now he was a middle-aged man, and she an elderly woman. He was a graduate of several penal institutions, she a graduate from the valley of the shadow. His last arrest and conviction were for a crime in which he implicated his mother. Though long since he had reduced her to poverty, until this time he had left her good name unsmirched. But finally he tried to destroy even that. And still the mother kept praying.

During the last few weeks of her earthly life, the mother had a visitor. The Chaplain from the penitentiary travelled a long distance to tell that her son had died. But his was a glorious death. Driven by boredom he had gone to the barren prison chapel, where he heard, perhaps for the thousandth time, the message that Jesus Christ went to a cross to save men. And Jesus said, "If any man will come after me, let him deny himself, and take up his cross, and follow me" (Matthew 16:24). For the first time in almost fifty years, the convict really heard the gospel. He who so long had denied Christ determined to travel with Him. Then the question rose: How can a man in prison take up the cross?

One morning the guard read an announcement. Volunteers were needed to accept inoculation by the virus of a little-understood disease. With the announcement was a double warning. First, the disease often is fatal. Second, if the volunteer survived, he could expect at the most one month's shortening of his sentence. With these warnings firmly in mind, the convict volunteered. He contracted the dread disease, and he died.

Because he gave his life, the doctors learned some of the answers they had long been seeking. A lifetime's prayers were answered. The mother lost a scoundrel, but she gained a man. "Greater love hath no man than this, that a man lay down his life for his friend."

Perhaps, if you have a vivid imagination, you can picture worse tragedies than the ones described, but surely these are tragic enough. In each is an evil that brought untold disappointment to someone. But in each the Spirit of the living Christ enabled a Christian to face disaster courageously, with dignity, and in the end, triumphantly.

Christians believe in God the Holy Spirit, God-in-the-world. We find Him in nature, in beauty, in love, in work. But Christians go even farther. We seek and find Him in the heart of life's major tragedies.

We . . . rejoice in hope of the glory of God. And not only so, but we glory in tribulations also: knowing that tribulation worketh patience; and patience, experience; and experience, hope; and hope maketh not ashamed; because the love of God is shed abroad in our hearts by the Holy Ghost which is given unto us.

Romans 5:2-5

9

THE DIFFERENCE FAITH MAKES

In Time of Tension

When Peter was come up to Jerusalem, they that were of the circumcision contended with him, saying, Thou wentest in to men uncircumcised, and didst eat with them. But Peter rehearsed the matter from the beginning, and expounded it by order unto them, saying, I was in the city of Joppa praying: and in a trance I saw a vision, A certain vessel descend, as it had been a great sheet, let down from heaven by four corners; and it came even to me: upon the which when I had fastened mine eyes, I considered, and saw fourfooted beasts of the earth, and wild beasts, and creeping things, and fowls of the air. And I heard a voice saying unto me, Arise, Peter; slay and eat. But I said, Not so, Lord: for nothing common or unclean hath at any time entered into my mouth. But the voice answered me again from heaven, What God hath cleansed, that call not thou common. And this was done three times: and all were drawn up again into heaven. And, behold, immediately there were three men

*already come unto the house where I was,
sent from Caesarea unto me. And the Spirit bade
me go with them, nothing doubting. Moreover
these six brethren accompanied me, and we
entered into the man's house: and he shewed
us how he had seen an angel in his house,
which stood and said unto him, Send men to
Joppa, and call for Simon, whose surname is
Peter; who shall tell thee words, whereby
thou and all thy house shall be saved. And as I
began to speak, the Holy Ghost fell on them,
as on us at the beginning. Then remembered I
the word of the Lord, how that he said,
John indeed baptized with water; but ye shall
be baptized with the Holy Ghost. Forasmuch
then as God gave them the like gift as he did
unto us, who believed on the Lord Jesus Christ;
what was I, that I could withstand God? When
they heard these things, they held their peace,
and glorified God, saying, Then hath God also
to the Gentiles granted repentance unto life.*

ACTS 11:2-18

In the passage quoted above one can see clearly how
the Holy Spirit guided the Apostle Peter into the
correct solution to a critical problem. In a less spec-
tacular way, the Holy Spirit was active likewise in the
lives of Peter's vocal critics within the home church.
The Spirit led them to gather the facts before coming
to a conclusion, to consult the facts and not their
feelings, to choose God's will rather than their own
desires, then, after discovering God's will, to act upon
it. In all this activity of the Spirit, the human agents

felt no sudden, special surge of divine power and influence. The Holy Spirit worked through consciences made sensitive by faith, and through orderly, logical thought.

The Church in a Divided Society

It is difficult for us to understand the physical revulsion that many ancient Jews had toward the idea of eating with Gentiles. To us, it would seem startling that Peter should baptize a person outside the Jewish community of faith. To his contemporaries, the complaint was that he had eaten with such a person. Apparently they were willing that Gentiles should be "saved" in a distant, antiseptic sort of way, but they did not desire any real fellowship with them, saved or not.

From the perspective of history, we can see the major problem clearly. The central issue of first century Christianity was the relationship with Hebrew faith. Should Christianity remain a Jewish sect, like the Sadducees or the Essenes? Or should the Christian church launch out independently? Underlying the practical question is the theological issue: Is Jesus the best of the prophets, or did God become incarnate in Him? We who know how the struggle came out are likely to be critical of the Jewish party in the early church. Before condemning them, we had better try to understand their side of the problem. After all, they took the trouble to understand our side, and when they understood it, they voted in our favor.

Jesus was an orthodox Jew. All His disciples were orthodox Jews, and so (we believe) were the five hundred who witnessed the resurrection and the three thousand who were baptized on the first Christian Pentecost. The Jewish people had lived with a problem for the past thousand years or so, of maintaining the pure faith in a world that is far from pure. Though some measures they adopted seem harsh and repressive to us, we should remember that they held to the faith when it would have been expedient to go along with the culture patterns of the day. It was easy for the light of faith to flicker out in the darkness of polytheism. The solution that worked best, in the ancient world, was isolation. A Jewish business man could trade with anyone, regardless of his religion. But in his social and religious life, the Jew kept strictly with his fellow Jews.

Peter was led by the Spirit to the home of Cornelius, a Roman army officer. The hospitable centurion offered Peter a meal, and he accepted. Possibly this meal was the first non-kosher food he ever had eaten. He was making a grave break with tradition, and he knew it. Then Peter told a group of honest seekers, who had not come through a Jewish background, the glorious gospel of Christ. As he was speaking, there was some outward, visible indication that they too had been seized by the power of the Holy Spirit. Until the time of his vision, Peter had always considered Gentiles common or unclean. In light of the vision he could see that God had accepted these unclean people as His children, on the basis of their faith in Jesus Christ. They had not adopted the dietary laws of the Old Testament. Peter was forced to make a practical decision, "Who was I, that I could withstand God?" And with that he baptized the Gentiles.

The Jewish Christians in Jerusalem were deeply — and properly — disturbed. One should not lightly tamper with a tradition that has been a thousand years abuilding. But these Christians remembered to act like Christians. They gathered the facts, they examined the facts in the light of their faith, and they allowed the facts to overcome their feelings. To a strict Hebrew, the idea of dining with a Gentile was about as attractive as that of eating roast dog is to you. You know that people eat roast dog, and apparently thrive on it. But you have no tinge of desire to join them. So the Jewish Christians knew that Gentiles managed to survive on Gentile cookery, but they did not care to partake. Along with zeal for the pure faith had undoubtedly developed a degree of spiritual snobbery. Let him who is without this sin cast stones freely.

Here are the controlling facts: First, tradition, custom, and feeling are opposed to fellowship with Gentiles. Second, God has accepted Gentiles as His children. Third, if one is a child of God, through faith, then every other child of His is one's brother or sister. Something had to give way, and the past gave way to the future. A treasured tradition collided with God's will, and the members of the early church had the grace to rejoice when God broke down a barrier between them and the Gentiles. You can be sure that our fathers of Hebrew background felt quite squeamish about their first association with Gentile Christians, but faith in Christ overcame their qualms.

After the early church had stepped from the rigid bounds of Hebrew tradition, the members found themselves faced with the same problem, keeping the faith pure in a world that is pagan. Christians had to be warned, and frequently, against descending into the spiritual morass of paganism. But isolation is no solution for the Christian. The logic of Christianity demands a constant breaking through the barriers of society. If society is hostile to Christ, win society to Him.

Divisions, Benign and Malignant

In Christian terms, whatever stands as a barrier is bad. Yet modern society is criss-crossed with divisions, many of which are absolutely essential to civilization. Some people, even a few Christians, hold the distressing belief that God expects from man a dull level of uniformity, with everybody thinking the same about everything. As you explore the incredible diversity of God's handiwork in nature, you should be able to guess that He has not poured all of humanity into the same mould.

In the beginning God created the human race male and female. Though I once knew a Dean of Women who apparently thought the whole idea a big mistake, the majority of us believe that this central cleavage of society, with all the misunderstanding and friction it entails, still offers opportunity for the noblest and best expression of human love — the family.

You and I, like all right-thinking people, support the Cleveland Indians. Each summer our hopes rise and fall with the fortunes of the team. Incredible as it may seem, there are many in the country who differ from us. They cheer enthusiastically for the New York (ugh) Yankees, and similar mistakes. Though we try to win them from their stubborn fanaticism by careful, reasoned argument, they persist in being wrong about baseball teams. Perhaps it is fortunate for us that they do. If everybody wanted the same team to win all the time, in short order there would be no Cleveland Indians and no organized baseball. Our land would be the poorer without the friendly rivalry of athletics.

Many of us believe that competition between industries produces a better product for the customer, and a better standard of living for the worker, than would result from a more logically constructed order of business life. Industrial systems have been devised that look better on paper. But when it comes to producing the goods, healthy competition seems to solve many theoretical problems in a hurry.

As we look across the sea to vast nations where there is but one political party that informs everyone what to think and how to act, we can thank God that the people in our country are divided, sometimes sharply, into Democrats and Republicans. We have the recurring opportunity to throw the rascals out. Close personal friends can be bitter political enemies. The loyal opposition of the minority party strengthens the country, by exposing weakness in the program and plan of the majority party.

A thoughtful reading of church history, with its sordid record of the tyranny that can result when one church is dominant, ought to convince almost anyone that religious freedom is worth the high price of competing denominations, and loud shouts from the lunatic fringe.

Nothing said above suggests approval of any abuses that have developed in organized athletics, business life, politics, or the church. Certainly every Christian must blush for parts of the record, where Christians have acted like gangsters in settling their disagreements.

I am just pointing out that diversity is sometimes better than unity. Would you enjoy hearing a symphony orchestra composed entirely of trombones that could play only B flat? The majesty of the symphony rises from the harmonious combination of different instruments, each making its distinctive contribution.

It should be the elementary duty of the church to distinguish between the benign and the malignant divisions of society, to encourage the benign, and to heal the malignant. Since each malignant division has its own staunch defenders, the Christian will need a spiritual touchstone that enables him to tell the difference. He has that touchstone in Holy Scripture. Hark back to Galatians:

> The works of the flesh . . . are these: Adultery, fornication, uncleanness, lasciviousness, idolatry, witchcraft, hatred, variance, emulations, wrath, strife, seditions, heresies, envyings, murders, drunkenness, revellings, and such like. . . . But the fruit of the Spirit is love, joy, peace, longsuffering, gentleness, goodness, faith, meekness, temperance.
>
> Galatians 5:19-23

Both lists are "natural," that is, they lie well within the spiritual capacities of a normal human being. But the first group reflects the complete absence of love, while the second reflects the complete presence of love. Where love is developing, a division within society is healthy. Where a division leads to "hatred, wrath, strife, and sedition" it is malignant.

A Malignant Division in Society Today

The industrialists in Middletown have imported thousands of poor people from the hills to operate punch presses and riveting machines. These people are usually called "hillbillies." (Substitute "greasers," "crackers," "okies," or some other term if it will help out with the local color.) Let it be said at once, the worst hillbillies are fairly distressing. But the worst of the local product is nothing to brag about, either. The good respectable people of Middletown have extended the hillbilly the same cordial welcome they would give to a plague of locusts.

The farmer is not more virtuous, in this department, than his city cousin. In an exhaustive study, *Migratory Labor in American Agriculture*, a presidential commission has reported:

Migrants are children of misfortune. . . . They move restlessly over the face of the land but they neither belong to the land nor does the land belong to them. . . . The public acknowledges the existence of migrants but declines to accept them as full members of the community. As crops ripen, farmers anxiously await their coming; as the harvest closes, the community with equal anxiety awaits their going.

City or country, north or south, east or west of the Continental Divide, it seems to make remarkably little difference. Wherever you go, you find that in our society certain people are treated like things. Society does not care for them, except as impersonal production units. In our Christian way of life, each person ought to be treated as an actual, or potential, child of God.

It would be foolish to ignore the problems that rise when large numbers of hillbillies move into Middletown. Almost all of them come from backgrounds of poverty. They have never handled much folding money before. The resulting antics of a minority drive credit managers to the verge of insanity. Many have rather elementary ideas about sanitation. In their crowded slums, almost-forgotten infectious diseases develop and spread to the surrounding community. Many have little education. When their children enter the public schools, educational standards drop with a dull, leaden thud. These are grave problems that could be documented almost endlessly. The obvious solution to these problems is: ignore the hillbilly. Pretend he is not there. Maybe he will go away. This, apparently, is the solution that many Christian churches have adopted.

In Middletown is a large, flourishing Protestant denomination hereinafter to be called the Methyterian Luthiscopal Church. One downtown church of this denomination is completely surrounded by hillbillies. The members, one and all, come from several miles away. A hillbilly would not actually be turned away if he came to worship, but he would not be invited back. At a regional meeting of the denomination, a devout layman of the church explained this policy of exclusiveness. He said, "These people aren't Methyterian material, and they never will be." Though some of the younger Christians present were shocked at his apparent denial of Christ, the older ones were glad to hear it said in English, after so many years of being clouded in theological double talk.

Here is a division within a community. It is not based upon love, but upon difference in economic and social standards. It does not produce love, but fear, hatred, and snobbery. In Biblical terms, this division is "the work of the flesh," something to be overcome by the inner presence of the Holy Spirit. You would think the church would be aflame with desire to heal this malignant division, to solve the many problems that result when a hillbilly becomes a brother. There will be a short pause for laughter — though tears would be more fitting.

If only the world could be saved by passing resolutions, the world would have been saved long ago. At a recent National Convocation of the Methyterian Luthiscopal Church, the assembled fathers and brothers passed a vigorous resolution:

We believe it the duty of the whole church to present the claims of the gospel to all people and, as God offers opportunity, to invite and welcome into the holy fellowship and communion all who believe, without distinction of race, color, or worldly condition. This is an obligation laid upon us by the very nature of the gospel. God now offers an opportunity to our congregations to demonstrate the inclusiveness of our fellowship in Christ, and thus give an example to the world. Each particular congregation shall in its membership be an inclusive church, defined as a church which diligently seeks and welcomes into full fellowship and communion, without any arbitrary distinctions whatsoever, all those living within its area of responsibility, who, confessing their faith in the Lord Jesus Christ, are prepared to accept the privileges and duties of their faith.

Local congregations have taken the plunge into complete fellowship with all the majestic deliberation of glaciers moving across northern Greenland toward the sea. Is there anything wrong with the resolution that they thaw out and get moving? As resolutions go it has not a single flaw. It is sincere, Christ-centered, practical. It does not ignore the difficulties as it holds aloft the standard. Every major Protestant denomination in the United States has adopted some such resolution. Without exception, when the servants of Christ meet in national assembly, they vote like Christians. But somehow the long trip back home seems to temper their zeal. With Protestants, a national resolution is one thing; implementing it on the local level is another. Protestants cannot be ordered about, they must be persuaded.

The meat of the discussion can be reduced to a syllogism:

Major Premise: The Spirit of God is concerned to heal the malignant divisions that exist in every community.

Minor Premise: Malignant divisions exist within your community.

Conclusion: The conclusion is up to you.

10

RECEIVING THE SPIRIT

> *If ye love me, keep my commandments.*
> *And I will pray the Father, and he shall give*
> *you another Comforter, that he may*
> *abide with you for ever; even the Spirit of*
> *truth; whom the world cannot receive,*
> *because it seeth him not, neither knoweth*
> *him: but ye know him; for he dwelleth*
> *with you, and shall he in you.*
>
> JOHN 14:15-17

As the Teacher was saying good-bye to His class, He made a promise. "If you will keep my commandments, I shall. ask my Father to send another Comforter to be with you forever. This is the Spirit of truth, whom the world cannot receive. But He will dwell with you and be in you." The word "comfort" has had rough sledding during the past few centuries. Today it means "coziness" in English. What Jesus promises is rather the indwelling strength and counsel of almighty God.

The Spirit of Truth

It is important that Jesus describes the indwelling God as "the Spirit of truth." For many centuries now, theologians have been differing about the type of truth under discussion. Some say that the Savior means only "religious" truth. Some say that He means all of truth. I trust you are aware by now which side of this discussion I am upholding. It is a profound and important "religious" truth that six plus eight equals fourteen. We who believe that God created this world and infuses it must believe that, in the long run, every truth is harmonious with every other truth.

Truth speaks many languages. The late William Lyons Phelps was contrasting the truth of scientific statement to that of poetry, and he said: "With a scientific statement you have to ask, 'When was it written?' With the twenty-third Psalm, it doesn't make any difference when it was written." The twenty-third Psalm is not the same kind of truth as the statement, "The sum of the internal angles of a triangle is 180 degrees," chiefly because I am not a sheep. But today when mathematicians deny the truth of that statement about angles, millions upon millions of people, who are not sheep in any literal sense, rejoice in the truth (as well as the beauty), "The Lord is my shepherd." The selfsame Spirit who led David to compose the Psalm guided Euclid in making his discoveries about the angles of a triangle, and He is guiding other scientists into a deeper understanding of triangles, space, and reality.

There is nothing inharmonious about the truth of non-Euclidian geometry and the truth that "The Lord is my shepherd." A few quite vocal Christians have the odd idea that our faith is opposed to scientific inquiry. They are afraid that the God of truth might lead men

to discover something they do not like. There are pages
of history that do no great credit to our confidence
that Christ would send the Spirit of truth into the
world. But by and large the record is good. In one of
the most virulent attacks on Christianity I have ever
read, the author said that Christianity, by its insistence
upon truth, gave birth to modern science. He suggested
that since we have done our important work, we ought
to go out of business. Without accepting the conclusion,
one can notice that even our enemies must agree that
sometimes we Christians act the way we talk. In *Science
and the Modern World* Professor Albert North White-
head has shown that science is directly dependent upon
the Christian insistence that man lives in a world of
order, that there is truth, and the human mind can
know truth. These beliefs are matters of faith. You
cannot prove them, because all proof presupposes them.
Truth is now, and always must be, the basic concern
of every Christian, for the Spirit of truth dwells
within him.

The World Cannot Receive

People who hold some massively stupid ideas about
God have discovered some important truth about bac-
teria and banking and matters of that sort. Jesus said,
"The world cannot receive" the Holy Spirit. The
world, of course, means people who are trying to live
without Christ. And many citizens of the world have
gone far in the quest for truth. There is no Christian
multiplication table. The important truth in that brief
document was discovered long before there was any
Christian faith. And he who discovered it was led by
the Spirit of truth. Quite correctly, we speak of the

"inspiration" in a work of art. Yet some artists, whose work was inspired, led lives that were a direct denial of the Holy Spirit. The Bible ascribes all talents, skills, and virtues to the Holy Spirit. And these are not the sole possession of Christians.

When Jesus says that the world cannot receive the Holy Spirit, assuredly He does not mean that the Spirit had no influence on human life before the Christian revelation, or that Christians have any monopoly on His gifts today. Often enough, people who have no use for our faith put us Christians to shame by their dedication to the ideals we profess. Everywhere you can find among people some true ideas of morality, some dim consciousness of the divine, and many sorts of virtues and talents. On this level of common humanity, all have received gifts of the Holy Spirit, who has apportioned to each of us certain abilities or opportunities.

When the Savior tells us that the world cannot receive the Holy Spirit, He is drawing a distinction between the natural man and the redeemed man. Both were born "of the flesh." The redeemed man is born "of the Spirit," who originates and develops the new life. Frequently the Spirit is working with what we would consider unlikely material. But we believe that the Spirit has eternity in which to transform a spiritual infant into a mature child of God. And we believe that He will succeed.

Every churchman has been taunted about the contrast between X, who is a moral pagan, and Y, who is trying, not very successfully, to be a Christian. Is there any real justification for the taunt? A scientist does his utmost to make controlled experiments. As far as possible, he uses identical subjects, the same in heredity, size, and age, and puts them under identical conditions of temperature, pressure, and diet. Then he subjects one to a measured difference. If there is a measurable change in the subject, he has reason to think he knows the factor responsible for the change. Of course, X is a better man than Y. Look at the home that each came from. Look at the native endowment X has, and Y has not. Look at all the differences that lie beyond the conscious control of either. The sensible question would be: What sort of man would X be, if his wonderful talents were directed toward the highest goal of all? What sort of man would Y be, if his pathetic talents were not directed toward God? X has received many gifts from the Holy Spirit. But Y has received the gift of eternal life. This, the greatest gift, X cannot receive, for all his brilliance and charm, until he is born anew.

Language Barriers to Religious Thought

When you mention the "spirit of science" or the "spirit of adventure" you say "it." Unhappily, many people, when they mention the Spirit of the living God, use the same pronoun. But our Savior says, "Ye know HIM, for HE dwelleth with you, and shall be in you." Christians always describe the Holy Spirit in personal terms. Jesus spoke Aramaic, a Hebrew dialect. In that language, the word for Spirit is feminine, "she." John wrote in Greek, where the word is neuter, "it." Most constructive thought of early Christianity was done in Latin, where the word is masculine, "he." In modern English, those who are careful with their pronouns call the Holy Spirit by the masculine term. To say the least, the linguistic confusion that has resulted is considerable.

"He" and "she" are not accurate terms to use about God, for these are biological words. But they are almost infinitely better than "it," the word we use to describe rocks and stumps. Until someone invents a super-personal pronoun, "he" and "she" are the best available. Human personality is the highest known earthly reality. It is a reflection, however dim, of the ultimate Reality, who is God. To describe God with personal pronouns is dangerous. It leads some to believe Him a reflection of man, inflated to sizable dimensions. But what idea have we nobler and better than personality?

We can best discuss God in terms of the "I-Thou" relationship rather than "I-it." We have meaningful relationships with all sorts of wonderful things: music, science, sport. But far more meaningful are the relationships with people: musicians, scientists, athletes. In your attachment to "music," for instance, the attachment is all within you. But in your friendship with the musician, both contribute to the relationship. The Spirit of God is more like a human friend, who can love and be loved, than like any beautiful, wonderful thing. The personal pronoun is the best we have to describe the Holy Spirit.

Any words we use to speak of God are doomed to be inadequate. Still, some are more adequate than others. And to describe the Holy Spirit, Jesus' word "she" is far more adequate than our word "he." The work of the Spirit that we have examined has been creative, intuitive, giving moral strength in time of weakness, bringing order out of confusion, producing beauty, warmth, and love. This is what the philosopher F. S. C. Northrop describes as the "feminine component" of reality. In human society it is woman who brings life into being, who creates beauty and order, who possesses the warmth of intuitive understanding. A frontier outpost, logging camp, or any exclusively masculine society is apt to be barren and bleak. But when the women come, men convert their shanties into homes, they paint the walls and mow the lawns and plant flowers, and begin to act like the human beings God intended them to be.

Because Christians have traditionally understressed the Biblical teaching about the Holy Spirit, there has been a vacuum at the center of religious life, that people have tried to fill in many ways. The cult of the Virgin that has developed in many countries springs from a basic human need to know, to love, and to worship the Holy Spirit. We need beauty, warmth, mystery, and color in our faith. Christianity is not only doctrine and morality. These without inward love are harsh and bleak. To neglect this "feminine component" of faith is "grieving the Holy Spirit" just as truly as neglecting morality or sound doctrine.

Dr. F. S. C. Northrop, in speaking of the comprehensive faith that is needed, says:

> This entails that the Virgin Mary representing the emotional female aesthetic principle in things becomes as divine in her own right, after the actual practice in Chartres Cathedral and Guadalupe, as is the Christ representing the unseen male rational principle in the nature of things.

> *The Meeting of East and West,*
> New York, The MacMillan Company, 1946,
> p. 455 (with permission)

Much as I disagree with the proffered therapy, I believe that Dr. Northrop has accurately diagnosed the weakness in much Protestant worship today. We do not need to create a new divinity. We say that the Holy Spirit is God. The time is long overdue for us to act as if we meant it.

Receiving the Holy Spirit

How does one receive the Holy Spirit? How does the timeless enter time to transform life? You would think it almost unnecessary to ask the question, since Jesus has so clearly answered it, "If ye love me, keep my commandments, and I will pray the Father and he shall give you another Comforter that she may abide with you forever." But evidently Jesus' approach is too difficult. Many improvements have been offered. Of course there is one troublesome question that we should ask about any proffered improvement: Does it produce better results?

Fads. One evening I attended a dinner where I was seated beside a woman who ate nothing but whole-wheat bread and celery. As she crunched through the meal, she remarked: "An increasing number of people are thinking about religion in terms of diet today." Perhaps unwisely, I answered, "Yes, that's much easier than thinking in terms of God." She appeared to be annoyed. There is a small, but audible, number of those who think that by following a diet, or some comparable fad, one can achieve the goal of human striving. It is easier to subsist on yogurt and blackstrap molasses than to follow the commandments of Jesus. But it is questionable that it enables one to attain the kingdom of God. Certainly a sensible diet is a part of Christian faith. But substituting the part for the whole is idolatry.

Emotionalism. Some in our country believe that the Holy Spirit is received only in ecstatic emotional states. They express their emotion with overt bodily motions and a considerable volume of sound. It scarcely needs saying that many of these people are the salt of the earth, who are striving fully to keep Christ's commandments. But when they say theirs is the only way, or even the best way, to worship God, one must disagree. To say that the Holy Spirit is present only when people are excited seems a curious limitation for man to place upon almighty God.

A staunch advocate of the emotionalistic school of thought once asked me, "Do you believe in the baptism of the Holy Spirit?" I answered, "Of course I do." He asked, "Then why don't you shout and dance in church?" I said, "Because I believe in the baptism of the Holy Spirit. I jump up and yell at football games, but when I worship God emotion goes too deep to be expressed in extravagant outward forms. I believe in the Holy Spirit, who tells us to worship in the beauty of holiness. There is precious little beauty in emotion without restraint. The Spirit tells us to do all things decently and in order. I believe I shall try to continue worshipping God in an orderly fashion."

I believe that my answer was technically correct. Yet I know that often the emotion of Protestant worship is so deep as to be undetectable. Much religious exercise is rather like worshipping God through a telescope. Some Protestants have put so high a value on restraint that their churches resemble walk-in refrigerators. Not only should we worship God beyond the farthest stars, we should seek him in the warmth and jostle of the crowd, the love that fills the home, the search for truth and the emergence of beauty. Certainly warmth, love, and beauty should fill the house of God. These too are works of the Holy Spirit.

I once knew a woman who loudly proclaimed that she was filled with holiness. When she shouted "Hallelujah," windows rattled on the other side of town. Yet in all the years I knew her, I never heard her say a kind word about anyone. She was not a stupid person, by any means. She could point out the faults in her neighbors with astonishing accuracy. These she would then contrast with her own virtues, sometimes for hours at a time. Once I read two and one half chapters of a long book while she was telling me about my sins, over the telephone. The emotion with which she worshipped God was genuine, intense, and audible. But in the eyes of her neighbors it was seldom expressed in charity. And what connection had it with the Spirit of Christ?

Organization. The other answer that one is likely to hear is "The laying on of hands." Our friends of the Roman Catholic Church believe that the effectual saving power of the Holy Spirit is transmitted down through the church by the laying on of hands. I certainly do not side with those Protestants who think their insistence upon decency and order a lot of mumbo-jumbo. It is important in every human society, including the church, that everyone know who is responsible for what. Protestants would do well to pay

more attention to form and structure than has sometimes been the case. But to say that the Holy Spirit can
operate only in a particular succession of the laying on
of hands seems another curious human denial that God
is almighty.

The structure of the church is important. Yet by
itself organization or structure cannot save. Take as
the classic example Torquemada, the Cardinal Inquisi-
tor. He was properly baptized, properly confirmed,
properly ordained, properly elevated to the high office
of bishop, and then properly invested with the rank of
cardinal. All was done decently and in order. The right
hands were laid on his head at the right times in his
life. And seldom in history has there been a man
farther from the Spirit of Christ. Unlike the human
monsters in our age, he carried out his tortures in the
name of Jesus. One could find in the records of Prot-
estantism similar examples of those who have totally
rejected the Spirit, in the name of organized Christianity. Organization is a good and necessary expression
of Christian faith. But it makes a remarkably poor
substitute for the Holy Spirit.

"If ye love me, ye will keep my commandments, and
I will pray the Father and he shall give you another
Comforter that she may abide with you forever." The
commandments of Christ are not easy. Far from it. Yet,
as you strive to keep His commandments, the indwelling God strengthens you. As you are striving the Spirit
of truth opens your eyes so that you can see clearly the
meaning of Christ's commandments in terms of today.
When you fail, the Comforter gives you strength and
courage and resolution to start trying again. This is no

distant divinity beyond the clouds. Jesus says, "She dwelleth with you and shall be in you."

11

THE SPIRIT, THE SON, AND THE FATHER

> *. . . the Holy Ghost,*
> *whom the Father will send*
> *in my name. . . .*
>
> JOHN 14:26

Glory be to the Father, and to the Son, and to the Holy Ghost, as it was in the beginning, is now and ever shall be, world without end. Amen. Amen.

So Christians sing or chant when we assemble to worship. Why do we sing these words? Partly because they have acquired a nimbus of hallowed association. They have become channel markers, to show that we are in the mainstream of Christian thought. Of course there is grave danger with any religious formula, that it may become a quaint relic of the past, cherished for its antiquity rather than its truth. Christians have demonstrated some, though scarcely enough, ability to discard the outworn words and concepts of the faith. But this concept is far from being worn out. We cling tenaciously to it; for it expresses something that cannot otherwise be expressed.

The Problem to Be Solved

Christianity is not a riddle to be solved, but a life
to be lived. However, we who attempt to live this
Christian life were created rational beings. As such we
must think about the meaning of our faith. Though
our faith goes beyond what can be proved, and though
it embraces mysteries where no logical explanation is
possible, still it remains our duty to explain as reason-
ably as we can those aspects of Christianity that can be
explained. We believe that the Father is God, and the
Son is God, and the Spirit is God, yet there are not
three gods but one God. Our belief is summarized in
the word "Trinity." This is a compound that means
tri-unity, the oneness of the three. Our faith includes
many difficulties, but no absurdities. No words can
remove the difficulty from the belief, but perhaps they
can dispel the impression that it is absurd. In what
follows, I hope to show where the difficulty lies, and
where many mistakenly think it lies.

The Christian faith affirms that God is one. In a
day of widespread polytheism, God opened His heart
to various chosen persons, and showed them that God
is one. In the course of time a Man came to earth,
whom men of faith hailed as God. There is no in-
soluble logical problem here. If one believes that God
is almighty, or anywhere near almighty, then it is
possible that He should come to earth in human form.
But the minute you give careful attention to the God-
man's teaching, you discover the problem. Little of the
Savior's teaching concerns Himself. Mostly He speaks
about the Father. Occasionally He alludes to the Spirit.

The Father is God. The Spirit is God. He who speaks is God.

It would not be difficult to find one of the world's religions that believes in three Gods. A devotee of this faith would think our difficulties with the doctrine of the Trinity quite irrational. He would say, "You have no problem. You believe in three gods, just as I do. I have my names for them. You call them Father, Son, and Holy Ghost." We Christians like to be agreeable, but here we cannot agree. Our belief lies betwixt two extremes, either of which is wrong. One extreme is tri-theism, the belief that there are three gods who happen to be on good terms most of the time. The opposite error is "modalism," the belief that the Trinity means only three different modes of thinking about God. If the modalist were right, the rest of the church would be wrong in singing, "as it was in the beginning, is now, and ever shall be," for the Holy Trinity would exist only in the human mind.

Long before the church had a carefully wrought creed to express the mystery of the one-in-three, Christians had known the glory of the Father, the saving power of the Son, and the indwelling strength and courage of the Spirit. It took centuries of thoughtful analysis before an unknown scholar was able to compress our beliefs into a concise statement. Today we call his work "The Athanasian Creed." It breathes the spirit of Athanasius, who lived and worked about three centuries before the creed was composed. Though this creed is inadequate, as any words are inadequate, it remains the best statement of the Christian faith in the Holy Trinity.

We worship one God in trinity, and trinity in unity; neither confounding the persons, nor dividing the substance. For there is one person of the Father: another of the Son: another of the Holy Ghost. But the Godhead of the Father, and of the Son, and of the Holy Ghost is all one: the glory equal, the majesty coeternal. Such as the Father is, such is the Son, and such is the Holy Ghost. The Father is uncreated: the Son is uncreated: the Holy Ghost is uncreated. The Father is immeasurable: the Son is immeasurable: the Holy Ghost is immeasurable. The Father is eternal: the Son is eternal: the Holy Ghost is eternal. And yet there are not three eternals; but one eternal. As also there are not three uncreated: nor three immeasurable: but one uncreated, and one immeasurable. So likewise the Father is almighty: the Son almighty: and the Holy Ghost almighty. And yet there are not three almighties: but one almighty. So the Father is God: the Son is God: and the Holy Ghost is God. And yet there are not three Gods; but one God. So the Father is Lord: the Son Lord: and the Holy Ghost Lord. And yet not three Lords; but one Lord. For like as we are compelled by the Christian verity to acknowledge every Person by Himself to be God and Lord: so are we forbidden by the catholic religion to say, there are three Gods, or three Lords. The Father is made of none; neither created; nor begotten. The Son is of the Father alone not made; nor created; but begotten. The Holy Ghost is of the Father and the Son: not made; neither created; nor begotten; but proceeding. Thus there is one Father, not three

Fathers: one Son, not three Sons: one Holy Ghost, not three Holy Ghosts. And in this Trinity none is before or after another: none is greater or less than another. But the whole three Persons are co-eternal together, and co-equal. So that in all things, as aforesaid, the Unity in Trinity, and the Trinity in Unity is to be worshipped.

Human wisdom has made no more precise statement of Christian belief than that. In the centuries that have elapsed since the Athanasian Creed was written, no one has succeeded in improving upon it. This statement, or any creed, is at most a map to be used carefully in exploring the mystery of the divine Being. Christians have been guilty of setting up creeds as graven images, and worshipping the idol instead of God. And in reaction against them, other Christians have decided that all creeds are worthless. The majority of Protestants believe that creeds are valuable human documents, to be used and interpreted solely in light of God's Word.

The Mathematical Issue

In an eastern university is a professor of philosophy who has written a book that nobody understands. This fact automatically makes him a qualified expert on theology. One day in his class, some students began discussing the mystery of the Holy Trinity. He listened in pained silence, but when the bell rang, he concluded the discussion by saying, "The Trinity is a mathematical impossibility." If the professor is right, Christians ought to know about it, the sooner the better. If he is right, though, it does seem a little strange that nobody within the church has noticed.

Christians hold to many difficult beliefs, but to none that are impossible. For example, as a part of my duty as a pastor, I ask people to believe that when they stand completely in eternity, and look back upon earthly life, they will thank God for every tear they have shed. Since my daily work deals with suffering that would wring the heart of a snapping turtle, you may be sure that I do not consider this an easy belief. On the other hand, I never ask anyone to accept such an easy belief as 6 x 8 equals 49. That belief is easy. Several of my young friends hold to it. Follow it, and you will not go far wrong. But despite its ease and general acceptability, I do not promulgate this belief. It is not difficult, but it is impossible.

One critic has called the Athanasian Creed "a vain attempt to vindicate by logical categories the harsh and irreconcilable antagonism of unity and triad." Unfortunately, a good many other people seem to find the doctrine confusing, on mathematical grounds. The genuine difficulties with this belief are not mathematical. Even so we had better pause and look at the meaning of unity. Then we can understand better what the unity of the three means.

What does "one" mean? The question is so elementary that few ever bother to ask it. Because people do not ask, they do not find the answer, and so even professors of philosophy are able to make ignorant mistakes. We are after the "one" of mathematics. You can point to one locomotive or one skyscraper. But the unity of mathematics is different. Whatever else it may mean, the "one" of mathematics is something that you cannot divide without creating at least two fractions. The "one" of mathematics has no constituent parts.

Look around the world for an example of "one." Take something simple. Take one apple. Count it. Then look at it more carefully. At the north end you have one stem. Surrounding the apple is one skin. Within is a mass of pulp. In the core are five segments. Within the segments are ten seeds. Around the seeds are ten casings. At the south end of the apple are the dried remnants of the blossom. One apple, upon cursory examination, turns out to be twenty-nine. But examine any one of the parts more carefully, and you will find it almost infinitely complex. It is composed of thousands, or millions, of cells. Each cell is many parts. Each part consists of molecules, each molecule of atoms, each atom of electrons, positrons, and a nucleus. The nucleus consists of neutrons, mesons, positrons, electrons, and neutrinos. At the present state of scientific knowledge, it appears that these are not stable, but transmute into each other. Where has the unity of our apple disappeared? Nowhere. It still has all the unity it ever had. Its oneness lies in the harmonious combination of many.

The "one" of mathematics has no actual existence. It exists only in thought. The "one" of daily experience is always a complex. It does seem a little harsh that we should permit "one" to mean "many" all day every day, but as soon as we start talking theology, we must make it mean something else. "The irreconcilable antagonism" between one and three does not seem to bother people much, except when they are looking for a club with which to belabor the beliefs of the Christian church.

How utterly complex is the unity of a human mind. Thought is not feeling. Feeling is not will. Will is not thought. Yet he who thinks, feels, and wills is one person. God has disclosed to us that there are three elements perfectly unified in the Divine Being, and each of these elements is a Person. The divine unity is dynamic, uniting into one essence the lives of the three. We need not think that because the elements of the Godhead are not sub-personal activities, but are Persons, the degree of unity is less than that of the human self. Quite the contrary. The unities with which we are familiar on earth, from the unity of an atom to that of a nation, are imperfect examples of the absolute unity, who is God.

Here is a mystery, to be apprehended by faith. Its truth cannot be demonstrated and proved. I do not mean mystery in the sense that spherical trigonometry is a mystery to most of us; for if we took the time, and if we had the necessary intelligence, we could learn all that is known about that complex subject. It is not so with the mystery of God. Those who know Him best, and have pondered the most deeply upon His nature, are first to affirm the absolute mystery of His being. The problem of the Trinity will not be solved by advanced mathematics.

The rationalizing intellect, of course, will not have it so. It will attempt to explain away the final Mystery, to logicize it, to reduce it to the categories of "this" and "that." At least it will attempt to water it down till it looks something like "common sense," and can be swallowed without too much discomfort! But the great theologians knew better. In the self-contradictory doctrine of the Trinity they threw the Mystery of God uncompromisingly in men's faces. . . . All attempts to make religion a purely rational, logical thing are not only shallow but would, if they could succeed, destroy religion. Either God is mystery or He is nothing.

> W. T. Stace,
> *Time and Eternity,*
> Princeton University Press,
> p. 8.

The One Who Is Three

Our fathers of the early church who formulated the doctrine of the Holy Trinity were not being obscure for the sake of obscurity. They used mathematical terms as the best available to express what man knows about God. The difficulty with the belief lies, not in their mathematics, but in the basic thoughts that are expressed. Many religious thinkers have decided that these thoughts contradict each other. To this charge, Christians can but answer, "Your God is too small." The Trinity is a statement of three fundamental beliefs about God. Many of the world's religions state one or another of these beliefs. Christianity affirms all three.

God Transcendent. Transcendent means "above" or "beyond." The Holy Bible is filled with vivid suggestions of God's utter transcendence. For example, Isaiah, a godly man, was carrying out his religious duties in the temple when he had a vision of God's awful holiness, and he cried, "Woe is me! for I am undone; because I am a man of unclean lips, and I dwell in the midst of a people of unclean lips: for mine eyes have seen the King, the Lord of hosts" (Isaiah 6:5). How strangely this attitude contrasts with the back-slapping familiarity characteristic of today's approach to God. A recent more-or-less popular song queries, "Have you talked with the man upstairs?" This easygoing chumminess with the divine is not Christian. When you speak to God as "Father," it should be with a catch in your voice, and with the knowledge that God has bridged an infinite gulf to enable you thus to pray.

An important thinker of our time has described God as "absolutely other," who completely transcends our earth-bound concepts and categories even more than the sun transcends the earth. All biological life on earth comes from the sun. Yet if you were to approach the sun in a rocketship, you would be scorched to a cinder, and your ship melted into a liquid projectile millions of miles before you reached the goal. He who made the sun transcends by far everything He has made. Our human wisdom, love, and goodness fade into meaningless insignificance, in contrast to His infinite holiness.

Christians affirm that God is transcendent. In recent decades, men have emphasized other truths about Him, at the expense of this one. Happily, the church is recovering the needed emphasis upon the unspeakable, solemn otherness that is God. Yet, when this truth stands by itself, it leads, sooner or later, into error. One error to which it gave rise, two centuries ago, is deism, the belief that because God is transcendent He has no dealings with the world. He created it, but after that momentary act, withdrew from it. This was the religious faith of Voltaire, Tom Paine, Thomas Jefferson, and many other brilliant thinkers. Thomas Jefferson is the only president of our country ever to write a religious book. It was not published during his lifetime, but was found among his papers, and published with them. This book is a treatise on the moral teachings of Jesus. It is a simple, beautiful account, moving in its humble reverence. Yet this book is one of the saddest I have ever read; for it closes with the words, "And he rolled a great stone before the door of the sepulchre, and departed." To the deist, God is too far beyond the world ever to roll that stone away, too distant to raise the Savior from the grave, too preoccupied to care whether or not people like you and me are saved.

God Immanent. "Immanent" means "dwelling within." When a Christian affirms his belief in the Holy Spirit, he declares that he believes in God dwelling within. Can God be at once beyond and within? There is the difficulty in the doctrine of the Trinity, not in the mathematics. Entirely too much Christian thought has considered God as the mechanic who keeps an engine more or less in repair. We who believe in the Holy Spirit ought also to think of God as the blood stream that keeps the body alive, healthy, and growing Christians believe not only in God beyond nature, but at the same moment we believe that God is within nature. We find Him amid the swirl and stress of daily life.

God is in nature. Christians have forgotten, again and again, that "the earth is the Lord's." The trees are sacred, the soil is holy, life is divine. Yet we tenants on God's property have butchered the forests and mined the soil, as if we were the creators and not the stewards. For example, we throw away daily tons of irreplaceable lead, by our adolescent zeal for jack-rabbit starts in the automobile. God has entrusted His bounty to us, and we squander it. Today the results of our wastefulness are beginning to overtake us, with tragic consequences. Nature does not belong to us, but to God alone.

> Not only are things brought into being through the agency of the Holy Spirit . . . they are maintained in being by the Holy Spirit. Not only is spiritual life maintained by the Spirit of God but material being as well. Things exist and continue by the presence of the Spirit of God in them. This does not mean for a moment that the universe is God, but it does mean that the universe is maintained in its being by the immanence of God in it. This is the great and solemn truth that lies at the foundation of the awful and debasing perversions of Pantheism in its countless forms.
>
> R. A. Torrey,
> *The Person and Work of the Holy Spirit,*
> p. 78.

Our Savior has told us, "Consider the lilies of the field"; for they can tell us of God's immanent power. We Christians believe that God is in nature. But when this truth stands alone, it becomes an error, in which "you wrap yourself up in the landscape and call it religion." God's immanence within nature, including human nature, is the profound truth upon which is based most of what we call "Oriental religion." We have no quarrel with the Hindu when he says, "God is in the stone." His error lies in stopping at that point. Exclusive emphasis upon God's immanence leads directly to pantheism, the belief that God is, quite literally, everything, or, in reverse, everything is God. It requires a strong stomach to swallow that last statement, but some have demonstrated this ability. The pantheist, having decided that everything is God, then concludes, "I am God." He thinks of his own personality as a temporary expression of the divine reality, much as a snowman is an individual today, but tomorrow will be melted and merged once more with the waters from which it came.

To the pantheist, Christian faith looks absurd, because it represents so much needless effort on God's part. Jesus Christ went to the cross, in order that man might be "at-one" with God. The pantheist thinks that he is already "one" with God. The distinction can be expressed with a very short word indeed. But let no one conclude that it is a trivial distinction. Man is not God. *God the Savior.* The distinctive Christian belief is that God is aggressor in man's salvation. Every religion offers a method of salvation, however that term be understood. In almost every religion salvation is man's achievement, through good works, prayer, sacrifices, or other techniques. By contrast, Biblical Christianity holds that man is helpless to save himself, that salvation is a gift from God. "When we were enemies, we were reconciled to God by the death of his Son" (Romans 5:10).

I have discovered many parallels to Christian teaching within the world's religious literature. But one teaching stands alone, and inapproachable. Jesus tells us to think of God as the Shepherd who leaves ninety-nine sheep in the fold, and goes out at personal risk to search for the one that is lost. This is Jesus' distinctive message, not only in words but supremely through a cross, that God is the aggressor in man's salvation.

To the one who carries belief in God's transcendence to the extreme, it is impossible that God should be our Savior. He is too far beyond the world to care. To the one who has carried God's immanence to the extreme, the pantheist, it is unnecessary that God be the Savior; for man is already God. It will just take a few more lifetimes in the flesh, and the soul can be reabsorbed into the All-soul. So, many would say, the belief that God is Savior directly contradicts the other two beliefs the Christian affirms when he speaks of the Holy Trinity.

Times come in life when experience gets ahead of logic. Christians know, by experience, that God is utterly beyond the world, yet utterly within the world, and that God is Savior. We have expressed the mystery of Christian experience in the word "Trinity." We recognize that our belief in the tri-une God is complex and difficult, that it appears to contradict itself. Yet any honest searcher for truth, when he finds data that are apparently contradictory, must affirm what he finds, and seek for the higher unity in which the contradiction will be resolved. That, as I understand it, is the state of physical knowledge today.

Experts can prove, beyond the shadow of a doubt, that light is an undulation. Then, starting from the same data, the same experts can prove, also beyond the shadow of a doubt, that light is not an undulation. Similarly, a proton is a particle; a proton is not a particle. Nothing can move at the speed of light; photons move at the speed of light. Logically, this state of affairs is absurd. Absurd or not, this is the state of affairs. Dr. Einstein was one valiant seeker who refused to accept contradiction as the final word in science. He sought, and believed that he found, a formula by which the diverse truths could be harmonized. But his formula was far in advance of the experimental evidence. Asked for evidence to support his conviction, he said, "I cannot believe that God plays dice with the world."

Perhaps the genius of Dr. Einstein has understood the mysterious inter-relationship of gravity, electricity, and light. But no amount of human genius will ever comprehend the mysterious unity of Father, Son, and Holy Ghost. It is no pious platitude when we speak of God as "infinite," without boundary. There is no outer limit to His holiness, there is no inner limit to His love. And the human mind cannot grasp the infinite. But knowledge of God is not limited to the intellectual. Indeed, Jesus told us that we must become like little children if we would know Him. And those who in childlike faith have approached the mystery have discovered, each for himself, that God is utterly beyond the world, yet God is completely within the world, and God is the Savior.